"/92

D0772615

A **H**ispanic
Heritage
Series IV

A guide to juvenile books
about Hispanic people and cultures

Isabel Schon

The Scarecrow Press, Inc.
Metuchen, N.J., & London
1991

OTHER SCARECROW TITLES BY ISABEL SCHON

Basic Collection of Children's Books in Spanish
A Bicultural Heritage
Books in Spanish for Children and Young Adults
Books in Spanish for Children and Young Adults, Series II
Books in Spanish for Children and Young Adults, Series III
Books in Spanish for Children and Young Adults, Series IV
Books in Spanish for Children and Young Adults, Series V
A Hispanic Heritage
A Hispanic Heritage, Series II
A Hispanic Heritage, Series III

British Library Cataloguing-in-Publication data available

Library of Congress Cataloging-in-Publication Data

Schon, Isabel.
    A Hispanic heritage, series IV : a guide to juvenile books
about Hispanic people and cultures / Isabel Schon.
        p.   cm.
    Includes indexes.
    ISBN 0-8108-2462-0 (alk. paper)
    1. Latin America--Juvenile literature--Bibliography.   2.
Spain-- Juvenile literature--Bibliography.   3. Hispanic
Americans--Juvenile literature--Bibliography.   I. Title :
Hispanic heritage, series 4.   II. Title : Hispanic heritage,
series four.
Z1609.C5S364   1991
[F1408]
016.973'0468--dc20   91-26335

To my parents,
Dr. Oswaldo Schon
and
Mrs. Anita Schon

to my husband,
Dr. Richard R. Chalquest

to my daughter,
Verita

TABLE OF CONTENTS

PREFACE

Like its predecessors, this book is designed as an aid for librarians and teachers who are interested in exposing students to the cultures of Hispanic people through books for children and adolescents.

These books are intended to provide students in kindergarten through high school with an understanding of, and an appreciation for, the people, history, art, and political, social, and economic problems of Argentina, Bolivia, Chile, Colombia, Costa Rica, Cuba, Dominican Republic, Ecuador, El Salvador, Guatemala, Honduras, Mexico, Nicaragua, Panama, Paraguay, Peru, Puerto Rico, Spain, Uruguay, Venezuela, and the Hispanic-heritage people in the United States.

A Hispanic Heritage, Series IV is arranged into chapters that explore specific countries and cultures, as well as one each on Central and Latin America as a whole. The books are listed in alphabetical order by author surname. These countries are representative of Hispanic cultures and should assist librarians, teachers, and students in their efforts to better know and comprehend the marvelous richness and diversity of the cultures of Hispanic people.

Although I have attempted to include most in-print books in English published since 1988 in the United States that relate to the countries and people listed above, as well as general books on Latin America, I undoubtedly have missed some important books. Their omission is due to unavailability, nonexistence at the time of compilation, or my own lack of awareness of them. However, not all the books listed are recommended titles. For the convenience of the reader, I have marked with an asterisk (*) noteworthy books. These books contain recent information, as well as being entertaining and possessing high potential for interest or involvement of the reader. I urge readers to be especially critical of many books that contain obsolete information or that expose a very limited or one-sided view of Hispanic people, customs, or countries. Students should be encouraged to read books that provide objective information and that present new insights into Hispanic people and cultures.

As any librarian or teacher knows, it is very difficult to assign a grade level to a book. And even though I have done so for the convenience of some teachers or students, please use the grade level only as a tentative guideline. An arbitrary grade level should never stop a student from reading or viewing a book that he or she expresses interest in.

In the annotations I have expressed my personal opinions of the books, emphasizing what I believe are the strengths or weaknesses of each. I have summarized, criticized, and/or highlighted specific ideas explored in the books about Hispanic countries and people.

In anticipation of user needs I have provided three indexes: an author index; a title index; and a subject index, including references and cross-references.

It is my hope that this book will encourage readers, librarians, teachers, and even publishers to expand their interests into the fascinating cultures of Hispanic people both in the United States and abroad.

I wish to express my appreciation to California State University, San Marcos, for its support; to the professional staff of the University Library, California State University, San Marcos, for their assistance; and to Ms. Yolanda Ramirez for her marvelous cooperation.

Isabel Schon, Ph.D.
Founding Faculty and Director
Center for the Study of Books in Spanish
    for Children and Adolescents
California State University, San Marcos
January 1991

A HISPANIC HERITAGE
Series IV

A Guide to Juvenile Books
About Hispanic People and Cultures

ARGENTINA

Argentina in Pictures. (Visual Geography Series) Minneapolis:
Lerner Publications Company, 1988. 64 p. ISBN: 0-8225-
1807-4. $9.95. Gr. 5-9.

This updated edition discusses the land, history, government, people and economy of Argentina. Numerous black-
and-white and color photographs enliven the sometimes dull
text. On the positive side, this narrative includes important aspects of Argentina up to the mid-1980s, which will
give young readers a basic understanding of this South
American country. It is regrettable, however, that the
editors chose to make the following absurd statement,
which serves only to perpetuate misconceptions in the minds
of English-speaking readers. They state: "Spanish is the
official language of Argentina. Argentine Spanish, however, differs significantly from Castilian Spanish, the official language of Spain" (p. 49). In the very next paragraph they state: "Buenos Aires is one of the world's
main distribution points for information printed in Spanish
and for many years surpassed Madrid and Barcelona in the
volume of books published. Printing and publishing are
still significant activities in Argentina" (p. 49). I wonder
if the editors believe that "American" English differs significantly from British English, hence books published in
the United States cannot be read in Britain. That is how
ridiculous their statement about "Argentine" Spanish is.

Carlson, Marifran. Feminismoi The Woman's Movement in
Argentina from Its Beginnings to Eva Perón. Chicago:
Academy Chicago Publishers, 1988. 224 p. ISBN: 0-
89733-152-4. $16.95. Gr. 9-adult.

The role of women as well as the feminist movement are examined in this readable account which begins with colonial times, continues with the movement for independence, the nineteenth century, and ends with Juan and Eva Perón in the 1940s and 1950s in Argentina. Readers will be interested to learn that despite years of struggle by dedicated feminists, women gained the right to vote in a few years through the efforts of Eva Perón, who "spoke contemptuously of committed feminists as masculine women of the oligarchy, castrating women who wanted to be men, false progressives who copied foreign ideas, snobs and cultural imperialists..." (p. 195). It is regrettable that numerous words in Spanish are misspelled, both in the text and in the bibliography.

Fox, Geoffrey. The Land and People of Argentina. New York: J. B. Lippincott, 1990. 238 p. ISBN: 0-397-32380-8. $16.95. Gr. 7-12.

The history, geography, people, culture, government and economy of Argentina are discussed in this well-organized narrative with numerous black-and-white photos. As opposed to other general introductions, readers interested in a more detailed discussion on current or historical issues will find this book more informative. For example, it includes an interesting three-page discussion of the city of Buenos Aires from a "big village" to a metropolis.

Juarroz, Roberto. Vertical Poetry. Translated by W. S. Merwin. San Francisco: North Point Press, 1988. 161 p. ISBN: 0-86547-307-2. $8.95. Gr. 10-adult.

According to the translator, this bilingual (Spanish/English) edition brings together a selection of the best poems by the Argentinean poet. Poetry lovers and advanced readers of Spanish will admire Juarroz's formal poetry, which is simple in language, profound and abstract in meaning and full of the mysterious possibilities of existence. Carefully done English translations appear on the same pages as the original poems.

Liebowitz, Sol. Argentina. (Places and Peoples of the World)

New York: Chelsea House Publishers, 1990. 126 p. ISBN: 0-7910-1106-2. $13.95. Gr. 6-10.

The geography, history, government, society, economy and transportation of Argentina are discussed in a most objective narrative. The author presents many positive aspects of life in Argentina today, such as its excellent educational system and cultural life. At the same time, he is realistic in discussing Argentina's future: "One question that confronts the Argentines is whether Argentina can avoid a return of dictatorship. Sweetened Peronism, offered by a new, charismatic president, Carlos Saúl Menem, may indeed be a turn for the better, but of course Perón himself sweetened his ideology before elections and then betrayed his own sugarcoated causes" (p. 113). The only unfortunate aspect of this book is the many blurred black-and-white photos, which detract from this book's potential appeal.

Peterson, Marge and Rob. Argentina: A Wild West Heritage. (Discovering Our Heritage) Minneapolis: Dillon Press, Inc., 1990. 127 p. ISBN: 0-87518-413-8. $12.95. Gr. 5-8.

The people, culture, geography, history, festivals and attractions of Argentina are described in a simple narrative with colorful photographs. The lighthearted tone of the narrative is exemplified in the following quote: "Argentina is a melting pot of immigrant peoples--not of different races as much as different nationalities. A half-truthful saying is, 'The typical Argentine is an Italian who speaks Spanish and thinks he's British!'" (p. 23).

BOLIVIA

Blair, David Nelson. The Land and People of Bolivia. New
    York: J. B. Lippincott, 1990. 208 p. ISBN: 0-397-
    32382-4. $15.95. Gr. 8-12.

The history, geography, people, culture, government and
economy of Bolivia are discussed in a straightforward manner. The author should be commended for candidly discussing difficult Bolivian issues, such as corruption in
government, an inefficient workforce, drug trafficking,
national debt and environmental dangers. Yet, he also
makes superficial statements such as the following that are
true only of a small number of Bolivian people today:
"Latin American women are not legally the property of their
fathers or husbands. Yet a Latin American woman who
takes up a nontraditional role risks the scorn of her family
or community" (p. 142). It is also disturbing to note that
the Spanish words "patróns" [sic] and "sorojche" [sic] are
misspelled on numerous occasions on pages 76 through 167.
Black-and-white photos, maps and charts are included.

Martin, Michael, ed. Bolivia. (Children of the World) Mil-
    waukee: Gareth-Stevens Publishing, 1988. 64 p. ISBN:
    1-55532-346-4. $12.45. Gr. 5-7.

This is a close-up view of how the very poor people of
Bolivia subsist. Through Porfirio, an Aymara Indian boy
who lives with his family on an island in Lake Titicaca,
readers will learn about the poverty, hard work, lack of
food, poor living conditions and other dismal aspects in
the lives of many people in Bolivia. Excellent photographs
in color depict the poverty and general shabby conditions

in the lives of Porfirio, his family and friends. The following are only a few examples of the many statements with their appropriate photographs: "Many people in Bolivia go to bed hungry" (p. 23). Discussing Porfirio's school, it states: "The children do not have any books" (p. 25). "Porfirio loves chocolate, but his parents can only buy it for him two or three times a year" (p. 35). The last fifteen pages provide basic information about the history, people, natural resources, government and modern problems of Bolivia, including the production and exportation of cocaine.

Morrison, Marion. <u>Bolivia</u>. (Enchantment of the World) Chicago: Childrens Press, 1988. 128 p. ISBN: 0-516-02705-0. $16.95. Gr. 7-9.

The excellent photographs in color (and a few black and white) of the people and country of Bolivia are the most valuable aspect of this introduction to the country. The photographs provide a true depiction of the landscape, natural resources and the people of contemporary Bolivia-- with noteworthy contrasts between city and rural life. The text discusses the geography, history, people, culture, politics, daily life and economy of Bolivia in a bland monotone. The basic facts are here yet nothing stands out. For example, not until the last two pages does the reader learn that "Bolivia is one of the poorest countries in the western world and has many problems" (p. 112). Even the illegal drug problem, though discussed, seems to be superficially treated. The last paragraph characterizes the overall mild tone of this text: "As perhaps the least developed country in South America, Bolivia faces an uphill struggle. A course has been set by the government. If its aims can be achieved, then the future could be considerably brighter" (p. 113).

CENTRAL AMERICA (General)

See also LATIN AMERICA and chapters on individual countries.

Alegría, Claribel. Woman of the River/La mujer del río.
Translated by D. J. Flakoll. Pittsburgh: University of
Pittsburgh Press, 1989. 95 p. ISBN: 0-8229-5409-5.
$8.95. Gr. 9-adult.

In a passionate and angry mood, the author, who was
born in Nicaragua, but considers herself Salvadoran, expresses her feelings against the United States' presence
in Latin America as well as her disillusionment about the
world. A well-done English translation faces the Spanish
version of each poem.

Bachelis, Faren. The Central Americans. (The Peoples of
North America) New York: Chelsea House Publishers,
1990. 110 p. ISBN: 0-87754-868-4. $17.95. Gr. 7-10.

Even more than other titles in this series, this one stresses
the abuse, exploitation and humiliation that Central Americans suffer in their efforts to immigrate to the United
States. It includes one chapter, ironically entitled "A
Legacy of Oppression," which briefly narrates the history
of Central America. Otherwise, it describes numerous instances of how Central Americans are constantly mistreated
in their search for a better life in the U.S. Generalizations, such as the following, may have a strong effect on
the reader, but they should be read as questionable exag-
gerations: "For many, the Mexican borders represent the
most dangerous part of the journey to the United States

because the border patrol is corrupt and unpredictable.
Migrants usually have to bribe Mexican immigration author-
ities, and young Central American women face the danger
of being sexually assaulted before they are allowed to enter
or leave the country" (p. 53). There is certainly much
more to Central American people than what this book depicts.

*Bierhorst, John. The Mythology of Mexico and Central
America. New York: William Morrow and Company, Inc.,
1990. 239 p. ISBN: 0-688-06721-2. $14.95. Gr. 9-
adult.

(See review under MEXICO.)

Black, George. The Good Neighbor: How the United States
Wrote the History of Central America and the Caribbean.
New York: Pantheon Books, 1988. 200 p. ISBN: 0-394-
75965-6. pap. $9.95. Gr. 9-adult.

Through numerous black-and-white photographs, political
cartoons, movie stills, travel brochures and an incisive
text, the author sets out to prove that "benign neglect
and extreme forms of crisis management have always co-
existed in the U.S.-Central American relationship" (p.
xvii). Critics of U.S. government policies in Central
America will agree with Black's condemnation of U.S. policy
beginning in 1898 in Havana Bay until Reagan's Costa Rican
peace plan in 1987. The news photos and political cartoons
are the best part of this "history" of U.S. relationships
with Central America and the Caribbean.

*Czernecki, Stefan, and Timothy Rhodes. The Time Before
Dreams. Illustrated by Stefan Czernecki. Winnipeg, Mani-
toba, Canada: Hyperion Press Limited, 1989. 80 p. ISBN:
0-920534-49-X. $14.95. Gr. 3-7.

A proud and boastful Central American shaman promised
the villagers that they, like all the creatures of the forest,
would be able to have beautiful magical dreams too. So,
he set to work and created the "Master of the Forest."
Since then, the shaman has remained a tapir and wishes for

the time before dreams. Simple, yet detailed, two-tone illustrations beautifully convey the theme of nature and
Central American lore in this charming tale about the creation of the jaguar.

Elections and Democracy in Central America. Edited by John
A. Booth and Mitchell A. Seligson. Chapel Hill: The
University of North Carolina Press, 1989. 214 p. ISBN:
0-8078-1843-7. $29.95 pap. ISBN: 0-8078-4249-4.
$10.95. Gr. 10-adult.

Eight scholars who have been working in Central America
"long before the Sandinista Revolution and the civil war
in El Salvador" discuss the question, What long-term impact
will elections have on democratization in Central America?
Serious students of Central American politics will be interested in this knowledgeable and in-depth discussion of the
meaning of elections and the democratic process (or lack
thereof) in Central America in the 1980s.

CHILE

Dwyer, Christopher, Chile. (Places and People of the World)
New York: Chelsea House Publishers, 1990. 128 p.
ISBN: 0-7910-1102-X. $13.95. Gr. 5-9.

Basic facts about Chile's history, topography, government,
people, economy and culture up to the late 1980s are presented. There is nothing particularly exciting about this
publication, and the small, bland black-and-white photos
interspersed in the text won't stimulate most readers' interests. The one aspect that is depicted with more verve
is the statements regarding Augusto Pinochet Ugarte's military rule. The following is an example of the author's
strong feelings against Pinochet: "In what it called a 'holy
war' against Marxism, the military junta arrested as many
as 90,000 people, or 1 in every 125 Chilean adults. At
least 2,500 people died in, or soon after, the coup; the
death total is probably closer to 10,000, although some anti-
Pinochet groups claim that it could be as high as 80,000.
Thousands more were tortured, threatened, or imprisoned
without trial. The mutilated victims were sometimes dumped
in rivers or left on street corners as a warning to others"
(p. 83).

García Márquez, Gabriel. Clandestine in Chile: The Adventures of Miguel Littín. Translated by Asa Zatz. New
York: Henry Holt and Company, 1987. 116 p. ISBN:
0-8050-0322-3. $13.95. Gr. 9-adult.

The Colombian Nobel Prize-winning author, Gabriel García
Márquez, records in a first-person narrative the secret
return of film director Miguel Littín to his native Chile.

The original plan, which proved to be quite risky in practice, was "to film an underground documentary on the in-
creasingly desperate situation in Chile after twelve years
of General Augusto Pinochet's dictatorship" (p. 2). García
Márquez interviewed Littín for eighteen hours and then
wrote this condensed account, which describes Littín's
experiences and thoughts during his two-month stay in
Chile. Littín, who "was convinced of the evil of the dictatorship" expresses his surprise upon arriving to the
capital of Chile: "Contrary to what we had heard in exile,
Santiago was a radiant city, its venerable monuments splen-
didly illuminated, its streets spotlessly clean and orderly.
If anything, armed policemen were more in evidence on the
streets of Paris or New York than here" (p. 16). Readers
interested in a personal account of Chile's contemporary
political climate will find this narrative exciting as well as
intriguing.

Garza, Hedda. Salvador Allende. (World Leaders Past and
Present) New York: Chelsea House Publishers, 1989.
111 p. ISBN: 1-55546-824-1. $16.95. Gr. 7-12.

This is a political biography of Salvador Allende, "the first
Marxist to become the freely elected leader of an independent nation" (p. 13). Numerous black-and-white photos
add a sense of relevancy to the life and times of Chile's
president, Allende, who died on September 11, 1973, at
the presidential palace--La Moneda--because, as the author
explains, "The CIA's plan had succeeded" (p. 19). There
is no question that the author blames Allende's death, the
collapse of the Chilean economy, and General Pinochet's
endurance on "the Nixon, Ford and Reagan administrations."
She also censures "the chiefs of six U.S. corporations with
extensive holdings in Chile--Anaconda, Ford Motor Company,
First National City Bank, Bank of America, Ralston Purina,
and ITT--[who] met with U.S. secretary of state William
Rogers and agreed to an economic blockade of Chile" (p.
74). Readers interested in a one-sided view of Salvador
Allende will surely agree; others will question and perhaps
dissent.

Haverstock, Nathan A. Chile in Pictures. (Visual Geography
Series) Minneapolis: Lerner Publications Company, 1988.
64 p. ISBN: 0-8225-1809-0. $9.95. Gr. 5-9.

The land, history, government, people and economy of
Chile are presented in a direct, objective manner. Numerous black-and-white and color photographs add interest to
this updated overview to this South American country.
The author should be commended for discussing controversial topics in Chile today with much insight and candor.
For example, in describing the military rule of Augusto
Pinochet, he states: "Much as they regretted the blood-
shed, many Chileans welcomed military rule. They hoped
that strong leadership would end the economic and political
disorder that had prevailed under Allende, who often had
exploited class rivalries between rich and poor to gain his
objectives" (p. 40).

Neruda, Pablo. Late and Posthumous Poems, 1968-1974.
Edited and translated by Ben Belitt. New York: Grove
Press, 1988. 239 p. ISBN: 0-8021-1078-9. $10.95. Gr.
10-adult.

Belitt, the translator of these late and posthumous poems
by the great Chilean poet Pablo Neruda, states that this
selection "will not serve as either a terminal or a compensa-
tory Neruda ... [but rather] ... to redirect attention ...
to an ongoing Neruda who took no notice of middle or later
or terminal chronicity" (pp. xi, xii). Admirers of Latin
American poetry will delight in Neruda's simple, clear and
forthright poems and the sensitive English translations.
The only disagreeable aspect, in this otherwise beautiful
selection, is that all the Spanish punctuation marks are incorrect. This is an inexcusable oversight in the publication
of the work of a Nobel laureate poet or any Spanish-
speaking poet.

Neruda, Pablo. The Sea and the Bells. Translated by William
O'Daly. Port Townsend, WA: Copper Canyon Press, 1988.
125 p. ISBN: 1-55659-019-9. $9.00. Gr. 10-adult.

These poems, found on Neruda's desk at the time of his
death, reveal his strong ties to nature and his love for his
wife, Matilde. Admirers of the Nobel laureate will delight
in these simple yet touching poems of a man who enjoyed
life and who could write about his imminent death. The
sensitive English translation conveys the spirit of the original

poems. Unfortunately, all the Spanish punctuation marks are incorrect. One has to wonder about the reasons for such a mistake.

Neruda, Pablo. Stones of the Sky. Translated by James Nolan. Port Townsend, WA: Copper Canyon Press, 1987. 75 p. ISBN: 1-55659-007-5. $9.00. Gr. 9-adult.

These thirty short poems, written by Neruda during the last few years of his life, reflect "a solitary observer of natural phenomena, detached, introspective, whimsically anthropomorphic, studying in great detail the living forms around him as if they alone could explain the meaning of his own life and death" (p. 2). Few young adults will be particularly impressed with this selection by a mature poet, but the bilingual format of this edition may appeal to a few unconditional admirers of the Nobel Prize-winning Chilean poet.

Neruda, Pablo. The Yellow Heart. Translated by William O'Daly. Port Townsend, WA: Copper Canyon Press, 1990. 109 p. ISBN: 1-55659-028-8. $17.00; ISBN: 1-55659-029-6. pap. $10.00. Gr. 9-adult.

Twenty later poems by the Chilean Nobel laureate, Pablo Neruda, are included in this bilingual (English-Spanish) collection beautifully translated into English by William O'Daly. In addition, it includes a comprehensive introduction by the translator that describes Neruda's improvisational spirit, his love of solitude and silence and the acceptance of his own mortality. Inexplicably to this reviewer, the Spanish poems are full of typographical errors and punctuation inaccuracies. As such, the original poems, as printed in this edition, leave much to be desired.

Timerman, Jacobo. Chile: Death in the South. Translated by Robert Cox. New York: Alfred A. Knopf, 1987. 134 p. ISBN: 0-394-53838-2. $15.95. Gr. 9-adult.

Timerman, a journalist who has lived in Argentina for many years, has written extensively about the abuses of power in South America. In his new book, he focuses on the oppressio that "emerged in September 1973 with the death of Salvador Allende" in Chile, which turned "into an army regime and then into a government dominated by Pinochet himself" (p. 8). In an intense manner, he relates the repressive practices used by General Pinochet's dictatorship to control the Chilean people. He states that the military has decided that "all women arrested for political reasons should be raped" (p. 30) and provides various testimonials of individuals who have been brutally tortured. He blames U.S. policy toward Chile: "the United States has run into a snag it has encountered many times before. The U.S. does not always know how to remove those it has placed in power, or whether it should do so" (p. 36). And, in a lighter tone, he states about the poet Pablo Neruda that "his longer, more combative verses not only are bad poetry but verge on the ridiculous" (p. 59). This is a strong personal indictment against General Augusto Pinochet's regime.

COLOMBIA

Bell-Villada, Gene H. García Márquez, the Man and His Work. Chapel Hill: The University of North Carolina Press, 1990. 247 p. ISBN: 0-8078-1875-5. $29.95. ISBN: 0-8078-4264-8. pap. $12.95. Gr. 10-adult.

Admirers of the great Colombian writer Gabriel García Márquez will be interested in this lucid examination of his life and works. It discusses the major forces that have shaped García Márquez's life, personality and political opinions as well as his short fiction and great novels from One Hundred Years of Solitude to Love in the Time of Cholera. A concise, select bibliography of major and minor sources adds to the value of this readable guide.

Colombia in Pictures. (Visual Geography Series) Minneapolis: Lerner Publications Company, 1987. 64 p. ISBN: 0-8225-1816-4. $9.95. Gr. 5-9.

The land, history, government, people and economy of Colombia are described in a direct and objective manner with numerous black-and-white and color photographs. Young readers who want an up-to-date discussion of modern-day Colombia will certainly find it here. Perhaps, one could object to the book's emphasis on Colombia's slums and poor people, but that, unfortunately, is one of Colombia's most evident realities.

Pearce, Jenny. Colombia: The Drug War. (Hotspots) New York: A Gloucester Press Book, 1990. 36 p. ISBN: 0-531-17237-6. $11.90. Gr. 5-8.

Through numerous black-and-white and color photographs
and a readable text, readers are introduced to the history
of the coca leaf; to the people, history and politics of
Colombia; and to conflicting views on how to deal with the
world's growing drug problem. Readers should realize
that this is not a book about Colombia, but rather it re-
views Colombia's problems with the coca trade.

COSTA RICA

Cummins, Ronnie. Costa Rica. (Children of the World)
Photographs by Rose Welch. Milwaukee: Gareth-Stevens
Children's Books, 1990. 64 p. ISBN: 0-8368-0222-5.
$12.95. Gr. 3-5.

Cristina, an eleven-year-old girl, lives in a mountain village in Costa Rica, where she works on her family's dairy
farm and in their small restaurant. Attractive photographs
in color and a readable text tell about Cristina's life at
home, at school and with her friends and family. In addition, this book includes fifteen pages of information about
Costa Rica's geography, language, currency, education,
culture, industry, political system as well as suggestions
for research projects and other activities.

Rolbein, Seth. Nobel Costa Rica: A Timely Report on Our
Peaceful Pro-Yankee, Central American Neighbor. New
York: St. Martin's Press, 1989. 253 p. ISBN: 0-312-
02262-X. $16.95. Gr. 9-adult.

The author states that he is "no Central American expert"
with "barely passable Spanish" yet he is obviously a strong
admirer of Oscar Arias Sánchez, president of Costa Rica
and recipient of the Nobel Prize for Peace in 1987, and
about many other things in this small Central American
country. In this lively, readable account, Rolbein describes
many aspects about Costa Rica's history, economics and politics, especially as they pertain to the U.S. It also includes
most flattering chapters on José Figueres and Oscar Arias
Sánchez. Some readers will enjoy his journalistic comments
on various serious and not so-serious topics, such as

prostitution, bullfights and Costa Rica's foreign debt. Others will question his final message: "... rather than taking this little oasis for granted, expecting a cowered subservience, threatening economic blackmail over policy disagreements, I think we should advertise and applaud Costa Rica as an outpost of the West" (p. 238).

CUBA

Sumption, Christine, and Kathleen Thompson. <u>Carlos Finlay</u>.
Ea. vol.: 32 p. (Raintree Hispanic Stories) Milwaukee:
Raintree Publishers, 1990. ISBN: 0-8172-3378-4. $15.33.
Gr. 3-5.

(See review under SPAIN: Codye, Corinn....)

Vail, John J. <u>Fidel Castro</u>. (World Leaders Past and Present)
New York: Chelsea House Publishers, 1986. 115 p.
ISBN: 0-87754-566-9. $16.95. Gr. 6-10.

Numerous black-and-white photographs and a concisely written text introduce readers to Castro and to Cuba. The
easy-to-read narrative and the captioned photographs present a mostly complimentary view of Castro and the Cuban
revolution. The following is an example of the author's
positive views on Castro as he reports on Castro's trip to
the U.S. in 1959: "With his tousled hair and shaggy
beard, dressed in his now familiar wrinkled, olive-green
uniform, the disarmingly eccentric Castro stood in favorable
contrast to the stiffly formal foreign leaders Americans were
accustomed to" (p. 66). The author avoids discussing
Cuba's serious economic problems of today but concludes:
"The Cuban revolution not only transformed the nation's
political and economic structure, it changed the quality of
lives, the attitudes of men and women toward each other
and toward their country. The revolution had a profound
effect on poverty, sickness, and illiteracy, and it altered
the way Cubans viewed themselves and their world" (p.
105). Some readers may find this biography useful and
informative.

*Vásquez, Ana María, and Rosa E. Casas. Cuba. (Enchant-
ment of the World) Chicago: Childrens Press, 1987.
128 p. ISBN: 0-516-02758-1. $21.27. Gr. 5-9.

Readers interested in an overview of the geography, history, religion, economy, and people of Cuba will find this
book most interesting and informative. A well-written text
and outstanding photographs in color and black-and-white
present an objective and up-to-date view of Cuba from
pre-Columbian times up to 1987. Maps and a "Mini-Facts
at a Glance" section make this book even more useful.

DOMINICAN REPUBLIC

Creed, Alexander. Dominican Republic. Edgemont, PA:
Chelsea House Publishers, 1987. 92 p. ISBN: 1-55546-
163-8. $11.95. Gr. 6-9.

This is a bland introduction to the land, history, religion,
government, economy, cities and other aspects of the
Dominican Republic. Most of the color, tourist-type photos
are quite appealing, but the tiny black-and-white photos
are blurred and overexposed. There is nothing in this
superficial narrative that will excite young readers.

Haverstock, Nathan A. Dominican Republic in Pictures.
(Visual Geography Series) Minneapolis: Lerner Publications Company, 1988. 64 p. ISBN: 0-8225-1812-0.
$9.95. Gr. 6-10.

The geography, history, government, people, and economy
of the country which shares the Caribbean island of Hispaniola with Haiti are introduced to young readers. Numerous black-and-white and quite a few color photographs add
interest to the informative text. Credit must be given to
Nathan A. Haverstock for presenting a balanced point of
view on the history of the Dominican Republic. Regarding
the U.S. occupation at the beginning of this century, he
states: "Although occupation caused resentment among many
Dominicans, the U.S. domination brought some material
benefits. High prices for sugar and cacao exports provided
revenues to pay foreign debts and the cost of occupation.
These revenues also helped to build schools and much-
needed public works, including sewers and roads" (p. 29).
And, about the dictatorship of Rafael Leonidas Trujillo, he

states: "Superficially, the country seemed to prosper
under his leadership. Schools were built, roads were
paved, and port facilities were modernized. Trujillo re-
organized industry and agriculture, but the resulting
revenues reached his personal treasury rather than that
of the nation" (p. 31).

ECUADOR

Ecuador in Pictures. (Visual Geography Series) Minneapolis:
 Lerner Publications Company, 1987. 64 p. ISBN: 0-
 8225-1813-9. $9.95. Gr. 6-10.

Basic facts about the geography, history, government,
people and the economy of Ecuador are presented in this
revised edition. It is unfortunate that many of the black-
and-white photographs are overexposed, thereby detracting
from one of the best aspects of this publication--its numerous illustrations. In addition, it must be noted that with
one exception, all of the photographs emphasize rural and
urban poverty in this South American country. The text
stresses Ecuador's economic and other problems with such
statements as "During Ecuador's first 95 years as an independent nation, it had a succession of 40 presidents, dic-
tators, and military juntas. Few leaders were in office
long enough to address national needs. From 1925 to 1948,
none of the 22 chiefs of state completed the term of office
decreed by law" (p. 6). There should be no question that
Ecuador deserves a more balanced view.

EL SALVADOR

Alegría, Claribel, and Darwin J. Flakoll, eds. On the Front
Line: Guerilla Poems of El Salvador. Willimantic, CT:
Curbstone Press, 1989. 89 p. ISBN: 0-915306-86-7.
pap. $7.95. Gr. 9-adult.

Twenty-nine bilingual (Spanish/English) poems by "Salvadoran revolutionists on the different fighting fronts of the
FMLN who have from time to time put aside their rifles and
taken up the pen to express the feelings evoked by the
cruel, bloody struggle in which they are engaged" (p. 11).
In a poignant manner, they tell about their fears and hopes
as well as their feelings against the CIA, among other political thoughts. (FMLN is the abbreviation of Farabundo
Martí National Liberation Front.)

*Argueta, Manlio. Magic Dogs of the Volcanoes/Los perros
mágicos de los volcanes. Illustrated by Elly Simmons.
English translation by Stacey Ross. San Francisco:
Children's Book Press, 1990. 32 p. ISBN: 0-89239-064-
6. $12.95. Gr. 3-6.

Based on the traditional Salvadoran tale about the magic
dogs that mysteriously appear at night to protect people
from danger, this modern version tells how the "cadejos"
protect the people who live on the volcanoes' slopes by
melting a regiment of lead soldiers. Bright, colorful illustrations complement the bilingual (English/Spanish)
text, which will be especially meaningful to young readers
from El Salvador.

Cheney, Glenn Alan. El Salvador: Country in Crisis. Revised
edition. New York: Franklin Watts, 1990. 127 p. ISBN:
0-531-10916-X. $12.90. Gr. 8-12.

Like its predecessor, this revised edition examines the political and social situation in El Salvador. Cheney stresses
the poverty, dismal living conditions and hopelessness of
most of the people who live in this Central American country. This book has several important weaknesses: The
black-and-white photos are neither original nor particularly
informative. Many of the words in Spanish are misspelled:
"mesónes" [sic] (p. 25), "Anastásio" [sic] (p. 58), "Demo-
cratico Revolucionário" [sic] (p. 61), "Napoléon" [sic]
(p. 63). And many will wonder about the author's obvious
support of the guerrillas over the military in El Salvador.
Repeatedly, he blames the military for atrocities committed
against the people. He states: "In several cases, the
military had bombed villages with artillery, shot at the
residents with machine guns from helicopters, and then
burned all the houses. Anyone caught in the village, including women and young children, was killed. In several
cases, babies were tortured in order to force mothers to
reveal the location of their husbands or sons. One refugee
reported the rape of children as young as eight" (p. 107).
Previously, he states: "Torture, which is still widely used
by the military, is rarely, if ever, committed by the guerrillas" (p. 49). In contrast to the first edition, this is not
an objective view of the current conflicts in El Salvador.

Fish, Joe, and Cristina Sganga. El Salvador: Testament of
Terror. New York: Olive Branch Press, 1988. 147 p.
ISBN: 0-940793-18-0. $17.95. Gr. 9-adult.

After "a number of visits to El Salvador," and personal
testimonies of Salvadoran citizens, the authors conlude that
the "fear underlying all other fears is that the U.S. has
shown itself to be so hostile to the idea of independent
change in Central America, and so determined to maintain
its control, that a revolutionary victory would in any case
attract more problems than it could hope to solve" (p. 116).
The Reagan administration and the government of José
Napoleón Duarte are, according to the authors, responsible
for the terror, destruction and human rights abuses that
are prevalent in El Salvador today. A strong, impassionate
narrative and numerous black-and-white photographs make

this "testament of terror," a one-sided view of a difficult problem.

Sanders, Renfield. El Salvador. (Places and Peoples of the World) New York: Chelsea House Publishers, 1988. 104 p. ISBN: 1-55546-781-4. $13.95. Gr. 4-8.

The history, typography, people, culture, economy and politics of El Salvador are discussed. The author stresses the disruption in El Salvador due to the civil war. If one reads carefully, one will learn that "Today, San Salvador is a modern city, with skyscrapers, sleek office buildings, wide streets, and large parks and plazas" (p. 73). Otherwise, readers will get a poor impression from reading this book and seeing the numerous photographs of poor, barefooted people in impoverished living conditions connected with statements such as: "sticks, patched together with mud, are used to construct many peasants' huts" (p. 27). As an introduction to the problems and poverty of El Salvador today, this book may be adequate.

GUATEMALA

Cameron, Ann. The Most Beautiful Place in the World. Illustrated by Thomas B. Allen. New York: Alfred A.
Knopf, 1988. 57 p. ISBN: 0-394-89463-4. $10.95. Gr.
3-5.

Juan, a seven-year-old boy, lives with his grandmother
in a remote village in the mountains of Guatemala. In a
simple, first-person narrative, the reader learns that Juan
was first abandoned by his father, later by his mother when
she remarries his stepfather who doesn't want him, and,
worst of all, he doesn't even have a bed to sleep on. The
sad realities of poverty in Guatemala are poignantly portrayed in this warm story about a hard-working boy and
his strong grandmother. Some readers may question Juan's
last thought at the end "... where you love somebody a
whole lot, and you know that person loves you, that's the
most beautiful place in the world" (p. 57), especially when
Juan has been abandoned by his parents and experienced
so much tragedy at such a tender age. Nevertheless, this
is an inspiring story that will affect young readers.

Cummins, Ronnie. Guatemala. (Children of the World) Photographs by Rose Welch. Milwaukee: Gareth-Stevens
Children's Books, 1990. 64 p. ISBN: 0-8368-0120-2.
$12.95. Gr. 3-5.

María, a twelve-year-old Mayan girl, lives in a village on
Lake Atitlán in Guatemala. Numerous attractive photographs
in color and a readable text introduce readers to María's
life at home, at school and in her village. Like other
titles in this series, it includes fifteen pages of information

about Guatemala's history, government, natural resources, education, and culture as well as suggestions for research projects and other activities.

Lattimore, Deborah Nourse. Why There Is No Arguing in Heaven: A Mayan Myth. New York: Harper & Row, Publishers, 1989. [32 p.] ISBN: 0-06-023717-1. $13.89. Gr. 4-7.

(See review under MEXICO.)

Volkmer, Jane Anne. Song of the Chirimia: A Guatemalan Folktale/La música de la Chirimía: folklore guatemalteco. Illustrated by the author. Translated by Lori Ann Schatschneider. Carolrhoda Books, Inc., 1990. [40 p.] ISBN: 0-87614-423-7. $12.95. Gr. 3-5.

This bilingual (English-Spanish) retelling of a Guatemalan folktale about a young man who tries to win the hand of a Mayan princess by making his song as sweet as that of the birds has definitely maintained a strong Mayan flavor. The bright, colorful illustrations beautifully depict Mayan traditions and customs. The easy-flowing English version reads like an authentic Mayan legend. It is unfortunate, however, that the Spanish translation is awkward and clumsy and lacks the spontaneity and natural rhythm of the Spanish language. It is indeed sad that young Spanish readers will not be able to enjoy this delightful Mayan legend, as translated here.

HONDURAS

Acker, Alison. <u>Honduras: The Making of a Banana Republic</u>.
Boston: South End Press, 1988. 166 p. ISBN: 0-89608-
336-5. $10.00. Gr. 9-adult.

The author, who is professor of literature at Ryerson Poly-
technic Institute in Toronto and is active in the Central
America Solidarity Network, has written a strong indictment of U.S. business and government policies and practices in Honduras. The first part of the book includes
an overview of the history of Honduras beginning with the
Spanish Empire up to the "Banana Empires." The second
part explains why Honduras has become "a beggar nation,
a sieve for international aid, a country for rent.... It
sits at the bottom of the Central American list in terms of
literacy, health care, nutrition, per capita income, life ex-
pectancy, and unemployment" (p. 11). Although Acker
states in the introduction that "Blame must be shared by
those who have governed Honduras, and by other nations
and business enterprises that have taken an interest in
Honduras" (p. 11), she is especially critical of the U.S.
connection and influence, which have "increased the military's political power, encouraged its abuse of human
rights, and catered to its veniality" (p. 120). Readers
interested in finding fault with the U.S. will find much
evidence here.

LATIN AMERICA (General)

See also CENTRAL AMERICA and chapters on individual countries.

*Ades, Dawn. Art in Latin America: The Modern Era, 1820–1980. New Haven, CT: Yale University Press, 1989. 361 p. ISBN: 0-300-04456-5. $50.00. Gr. 10-adult.

Latin American art from the years of the Independence movements around the 1820s up to the present is beautifully presented in this exquisite publication, which was prepared for an exhibition at the Hayward Gallery in London in May 1989. It explores "thematically and historically the emergence of what may be called a Latin America aesthetic and the questions of national and cultural identity associated with it" (p. ix). The well-documented and comprehensive text, as well as the fine color and black-and-white illustrations, makes this an excellent source for readers interested in Latin American art, especially Mexican artists and Mexican artistic developments. It also includes brief biographies of artists and translations of avant-garde manifestos. Inexplicably, it lacks an index and an exhibition checklist.

Agosin, Marjorie, ed. Landscapes of a New Land: Fiction by Latin American Women. Translated from Spanish. Buffalo, NY: White Pine Press, 1989. 194 p. ISBN: 0-934834-96-2. pap. $10.00. Gr. 9-adult.

Twenty-one short stories written by twentieth-century female authors from Latin America are included in this anthology. The editor states that the "idea for this collection arose from the pressing need to rescue the voices of the great women of letters that are scarcely known in English" and to "show the wide range of themes, images, and uses of language encountered in the new territories of the Latin American narrative written by women" (p. 2). Some of the authors represented are Dora Alonso (Cuba), Margo Glantz and Elena Poniatowska (Mexico), Clarice Lispector and Lygia Fagundes Telles (Brazil) and Silvina Ocampo (Argentina). The stories are divided into five sections: Genealogies; Destinations; The Open Letter; A Child, A Dog, The Night; and The Beguiling Ladies. Sophisticated readers may be interested in the thoughts, feelings and dreams of contemporary Latin American women as expressed in these stories about love, ancestors, prostitutes, servants and social/political concerns.

Baddeley, Oriana, and Fraser, Valerie. Drawing the Line: Art and Cultural Identity in Contemporary Latin America. New York: Verso, 1989. 164 p. ISBN: 0-86091-953-6. $19.95. Gr. 10-adult.

The authors state that the purpose of this book is to focus on certain artists whose work they feel exemplifies important aspects of contemporary Latin American art. Thus, they discuss "the shared history of colonial oppression, its twentieth-century legacy of continuing external interference and exploitation, and, in the face of all this, the persistent concern of Latin American creative artists to give authentic expression to their own voices" (pp. 1-2). Serious students of Latin American art and politics will be interested in these authors' views. Approximately eighty black-and-white and color reproductions of art works are included.

Barrios, Enrique. Ami, Child of the Stars. Illustrated by Glen Strock. Santa Fe, NM: Lotus Press, 1989. 113 p. ISBN: 0-914955-05-0. pap. $7.95. Gr. 6-9.

Through Ami, a ten-year-old boy from outer space, children are supposed to learn universal truths, such as the kindness of God and love as the road to happiness. There are definitely better messages about peace, love, contamination, self-destruction and other important topics than this "educational novel," originally published in Chile in 1986. As opposed to the original, it is interesting to note that this English translation does not mention Ami's residence--Chile.

Bierhorst, John. The Mythology of South America. New York: William Morrow and Company, 1988. 269 p. ISBN: 0-688-06722-0. $15.95. Gr. 9-adult.

This is a scholarly introduction to South American mythology written by a well-known folklorist and expert in the field. In a concise and lucid manner, Bierhorst introduces the reader to the main themes, motifs, and characters prevalent in South American myths by dividing the continent into seven regions: greater Brazil, Guiana, Brazilian highlands, Gran Chaco, far South, Northwest and Central Andes. This is not an easy-to-read collection of South American myths but rather a serious guide to the diversity of South American legends with a generous sampling from the stories themselves. Dedicated readers of mythology will rejoice and appreciate this well-organized and informative book.

*Civilizations of the Americas. (History of the World) Milwaukee: Raintree Publishers, 1989. 80 p. ISBN: 0-8172-3306-7. $15.50. Gr. 4-6.

The early civilizations of North, Central and South America are introduced to young readers through bright, colorful illustrations and brief texts. This is not an in-depth description of these civilizations, but rather a well-done overview of basic facts about early civilizations from Alaska to Tierra del Fuego. This series was originally published in Milan, Italy, in 1987.

*Day, Holliday T., and Hollister Sturges. Art of the Fantastic: Latin America, 1920-1987. Indianapolis: Indianapolis Museum of Art, 1987. 302 p. ISBN: 0-936260-19-X. $30.00. Gr. 9-adult.

The extensive use of fantastic imagery since 1920 by 29 Latin American painters is beautifully demonstrated in this exhibition catalog. Serious art devotees and interested readers will find informative essays on this history of Latin American art, as well as critical discussions on the artists' lives and works both from a North American and a Latin American perspective. The excellent color reproductions are a fine complement to this comprehensive view of twentieth-century Latin American art. Some of the well-known artists included are Frida Kahlo, Rufino Tamayo, Wilfredo Lam, and Alberto Gironella.

*Delacre, Lulu, ed. Arroz con Leche: Popular Songs and Rhymes from Latin America. Illustrated by the author. English lyrics by Elena Paz. Musical arrangements by Ana-María Rosado. New York: Scholastic Inc., 1989. 32 p. ISBN: 0-590-41887-4. $12.95. Gr. PK-3.

Twelve well-known nursery rhymes and children's songs from Mexico, Puerto Rico and Argentina are included in this delightful bilingual collection. The soft pastel illustrations add a note of authenticity and charm to these joyous Hispanic rhymes. Adults will welcome the melodies to each rhyme which are included at the end of the book.

*Gaines, Ann. Alexander Von Humboldt: Colossus of Exploration. (World Explorers) New York: Chelsea House Publishers, 1991. 111 p. ISBN: 0-7910-1313-8. $15.95. Gr. 7-12.

The life and times of the brilliant German scientist Alexander Von Humboldt are examined in a clear narrative with numerous black-and-white and a few color photographs. Humboldt's five-year exploration of Venezuela, Colombia, Ecuador and Peru as well as his travels in Mexico and Cuba in the early 1900s provide the reader with a firsthand view of life in these countries. In addition, would-be-scientists will be impressed with Humboldt's contributions to geography, botany and climatology.

Georges, D. V. South America. (A New True Book) Chicago: Childrens Press, 1986. 48 p. ISBN: 0-516-01296-7. $11.25. Gr. 2-4.

Directly and succinctly this book introduces students to

various sections of South America, including the Andes,
the Amazon Rain Forest, the highlands of Brazil, the
Pampas and the southern tip. Simple maps and color photographs accompany the easy-to-read narrative. Young readers will be especially interested in the discussion and photographs of unusual animals found in South America.

*Jenkins, Lyll Becerra de. The Honorable Prison. New
   York: Lodestar Books/E. P. Dutton, 1988. 199 p. ISBN:
   0-525-67238-9. $14.95. Gr. 8-12.

Seventeen-year-old Marta Maldonado, her journalist father,
her mother, and younger brother are taken from their
home and jailed in a house in the Andes. Thus begins this
gripping novel set in a South American country where political abuses and government corruption abuse innocent
people who have no recourse to justice or personal liberties. Marta's personal dilemmas, the family's travails and
Marta's father's struggle with tuberculosis provide a poignant and powerful indictment of life in a terror-stricken
country. The author, who grew up in Colombia, states
that this "is a fusion of personal experience and invention."
Readers will definitely empathize and understand.

*Kellner, Douglas. Ernesto "Che" Guevara. (World Leaders
   Past & Present) New York: Chelsea House Publishers,
   1989. 112 p. ISBN: 1-55546-835-7. $16.95. Gr. 7-12.

This is a balanced and well-written biography of the revolutionary who joined Castro's movement to overthrow Cuba's
government. Numerous black-and-white photographs and
brief chapters make this an engrossing overview of the life
of this charismatic revolutionary, including his successes
and failures in Castro's Cuba, his role as a diplomat and
ambassador, his death in Bolivia and his legacy: "Che
Guevara's major success was his participation in the Cuban
revolutionary war. Despite his many contributions to the
Cuban Revolution, his subsequent economic programs, diplomacy, and guerrilla campaigns abroad were for the most part
failures. Yet Guevara himself served as a compelling sym-
bol of the dedicated revolutionary whose actions were always consistent and in harmony with his moral ideals" (p.
107).

Latin America and U.S. Foreign Policy. (Opposing Viewpoints)
St. Paul, MN: Greenhaven Press, 1988. 239 p. ISBN:
0-89908-399-4. $13.95. Gr. 9-adult.

The editors have selected a wide range of viewpoints that
discuss the following issues concerning Latin America and
the U.S.: Is U.S. intervention the cause of Latin America's
problems: How should the U.S. deal with Latin American
human rights conditions? Are Latin American revolutions a
threat to the U.S.? What form of government is best for
Latin America? How serious is the Latin American debt?
The objective introductions to each chapter and the diversity of points of view expressed regarding these controversial issues make this publication useful to readers who
are interested in brief expositions of complex problems.
Serious readers will prefer more in-depth discussions of
these issues.

*Latin American Writers, Vol. I, II, III. Carlos A. Solí, ed-
itor in chief; Maria Isabel Abreu, associate editor. New
York: Charles Scribner's Sons, 1989. Vol. 1: 446 p.
ISBN: 0-684-185970; Vol. II: 527 p. ISBN: 0-684-
18598-9; Vol. III: 522 p. ISBN: 0-684-18599-7. For the
set: ISBN: 0-684-18463-X. $250.00. Gr. 9-adult.

High-school students, teachers, as well as serious scholars
will find this panoramic view of Latin American literary
history a most useful and informative reference work.
Critical essays introduce the reader to the life, work and
literary contribution of 176 Latin American writers beginning
with the colonial period up to the Cuban writer Reinaldo
Arenas. Some readers may be confused by the arrangement of the authors in the three volumes--chronological
order according to their date of birth--and some critics
may question the exclusion of such notable authors as Isabel Allende. Notwithstanding these minor caveats, however, this is a marvelous analysis for English-speaking
readers to the splendid and varied literature of Spanish
America and Brazil. Other valuable features of this work
are a chronological table of political and sociocultural events
and a list of writers by country.

*McIntyre, Loren. Exploring South America. New York:

Clarkson N. Potter, Inc., Publishers, 1990. 207 p. ISBN:
0-517-56134-4. $40.00. Gr. 8-adult.

McIntyre states at the beginning of this exquisite large-
format publication that South America "has the biggest river,
the largest forest, the longest mountain range, the driest
desert, and the greatest variety of life forms of all the con-
tinents" (p. 7). So, through his striking color photographs
and his well-done personal introductions, readers are exposed to the people, geography, biology and history of the
South American continent. It is difficult indeed to find a
most beautiful collection of photographs on South America
than these taken by National Geographic consultant and pho-
tographers L. McIntyre.

Michener, James A. Caribbean. New York: Random House,
1989. 672 p. ISBN: 0-394-56561-4. $22.95. Gr. 9-
adult.

Michener's talents as a storyteller are evident in this fast-
moving collection of tales that combine compelling fictional
and historical characters as they struggle for economic and
political power in various areas of the Caribbean. Readers
eager for lots of action and adventure in a beautiful area
of the world with a smattering of history thrown in for ex-
tra excitement will not be disappointed. I find it most unfortunate, however, that many English-speaking readers will
be introduced to pre-Columbian and Hispanic culture and
people by Michener's narrow generalizations and gross over-
simplifications. For example, in his chapter "Death of
Greatness," which tells about the Maya, the one aspect
that is emphasized and described in gory detail is the Mayan
practice of human sacrifice. He states: "Whenever the
city faced a crisis that required immediate instruction from
the gods, the priests brought twelve naked maidens here
at dawn and tossed them one by one into the deep water
down there" (p. 35). And, numerous occasions in which he
describes a Mayan priest who "lifted his obsidian knife,
plunged it into the left side of the rib cage, drew it deeply
across, and while Bolón was still alive, reached in and
grabbed the beating heart, ripping it from its hiding place.
Bolón remained alive just long enough to see his own heart
placed reverently in the waiting saucer of Chac Mool" (p.
48). There are many positive aspects of Mayan civilization,

but readers will certainly not be impressed by them from
this account. The Spaniards are treated equally badly.
Michener constantly refers to "the inborn arrogance of
Spanish men" (p. 67). The following is his conclusion of
the chapter "Christopher Columbus in Hispaniola": "I see
the men of Spain who come to these islands repeating in
perpetuity the behavior of Colón and Pimentel--steal, abuse
the natives, place relatives on the king's payroll, think always of self and family, never of the general weal. It's
a bad precedent we've established here in Española" (p.
84). Yes, this is exciting, fast-paced reading, but at
least to this reader, it is also disappointing because of its
one-sided view of Caribbean history and people.

Morrison, Marion. Indians of the Andes. (Original Peoples)
  Vero Beach, FL: Rourke Publications, Inc., 1987. 48 p.
  ISBN: 0-86625-260-6. $9.50. Gr. 4-6.

The history, daily life, and especially the impact that the
Spanish and Latin American governments have had on the
Aymara and Quechua Indians of the Andes are discussed
in a simple text with numerous photographs in color and
black and white. In addition, it includes brief chapters on
the Otavalo Indians of Ecuador and the "mestizos" of Bolivia
and Peru. Young readers may not be able to understand
the strong emphasis of this book, as stated in the introduction: "This is a story of a people who have managed to
survive despite hardship and oppression..." (p. 6). And,
the conclusion: "Significantly, the truly successful mestizo
rejects his Indian background completely, and if this trend
continues, as seems likely, it is inevitable that in the future,
the pure Indian will no longer exist" (p. 43). These are
two most complex issues which are definitely not satisfac-
torily explained in this book.

Moss, Joyce, and George Wilson. Peoples of the World: Latin
  Americans. Detroit, MI: Gale Research, Inc., 1989.
  323 p. ISBN: 0-8103-7445-5. $39.95. Gr. 8-12.

The purpose of this guide is to introduce readers to the
culture, geographical setting and historical background of
42 "people" from Latin America. It is divided in two sections: The Old Cultures (which describes Mayas, Aztecs

and Incas) and Cultures of Today (which includes obvious
groups such as Mexicans and Cubans as well as other
people in Latin America such as Pemon and Xingu Park Indians). Unfortunately, this book is not very useful. It
is most inadequate as a guide to most of Latin America.
Most encyclopedias or introductory books provide as much
or better information on Latin American countries. And,
information on less well-known or "disappearing" cultures is
indeed sketchy. For example, the population figures given
for the Tenetehara Indians of Brazil are for 1948. The
tiny black-and-white line drawings are more appropriate
for tourist post cards and the tiny photos on Mexico are
definitely quaint--"a street vendor in a Mexican town" (p.
174).

Paräiso, Aviva. Caribbean Food and Drink. New York:
The Bookwright Press, 1989. 48 p. ISBN: 0-531-18231-2.
$12.40. Gr. 4-8.

The food and beverages of the Caribbean are introduced
through numerous outstanding photographs in color and a
simple text. Perhaps because this book attempts to do so
much, including an introduction to the Caribbean region;
its history; production, processing, distribution and selling
of food and other aspects that it necessarily has to slight
some areas of the region. And this is especially true of
the Spanish-speaking islands, which are indeed the largest,
and which are barely mentioned. Only a few dishes which
reflect the Spanish influence are mentioned and the two
most important ones are misspelled: "arroz con camerones"
[sic] (p. 26) and "maros y cristnos" [sic] (p. 26).

*Pascoe, Elaine. Neighbors at Odds: U.S. Policy in Latin
America. New York: Franklin Watts, 1990. 157 p. ISBN:
0-531-10903-8. $12.90. Gr. 8-12.

In a direct and straightforward manner, Pascoe explains
some of the basic differences between the United States and
Latin America and traces the history of U.S. foreign policy
in the region, from the Monroe Doctrine up to 1989. In
contrast to many books on this topic, one must commend
the author for presenting, in most instances, a balanced
view of the United States' involvement in Latin America.

The following, however, is an example of how easy it seems to be for most U.S. authors to be overly critical of the U.S. Regarding the Lodge Corollary to the Monroe Doctrine, she states, "Of far greater importance to Latin America at this time was the scope and nature of the growing U.S. economic involvement. Because that involvement tended to perpetuate Latin America's dependence on exports of raw materials and agricultural products, it discouraged the development of industry. Moreover, to protect its economic stake, it was in the United States' interest to preserve the status quo in politics and society--the supremacy of the elite, landowning families. This meant that poverty remained the lot of the vast majority of Latin Americans" (p. 75). Fortunately, the author doesn't take this simplistic position throughout her book. She does present many sides of the complex issues facing Latin America today.

*Pimlott, Dr. John, ed. <u>South and Central America</u>. (Conflict in the 20th Century) New York: Franklin Watts, 1988. 62 p. ISBN: 0-531-10540-7. $12.90. Gr. 7-12.

This is a well-done analysis of the many issues surrounding South and Central America in the twentieth century written by an editorial panel headed by a Senior Lecturer in the Department of War Studies and International Affairs at Sandhurst in the United Kingdom. It is interesting to note the authors' objectivity and detachment in discussing the involvement of the United States in Latin American affairs, yet they are much more circumspect in describing "the Falklands factor" which resulted in an Argentinian defeat by Great Britain. Numerous high-quality maps and photographs in color and black and white add interest to this serious discussion of "a troubled continent." Two of the six appendices are especially informative: one deals with the Latin American debt problem and the other with the drugs connection.

Alvarado, Manuel. <u>Mexican Food and Drink</u>. New York:
The Bookwright Press, 1988. 48 p. ISBN: 0-531-18199-5.
$12.40. Gr. 4-8.

Young readers are supposed to enjoy a "taste" of Mexican
food and drink through this introductory guide to Mexican
cuisine. Its positive aspects are its simply written introduction, which provides a brief overview to Mexico and its
people and the attractive, colorful photographs of Mexican
food and people. It is unfortunate, however, that with
only two exceptions, all the photographs show food being
prepared and sold on the streets of Mexico in most unsanitary
conditions. In addition, there are a few mistakes on the
text. A more appropriate title for this book would be
<u>Food and Drink of the Poor People of Mexico</u>.

Ashabranner, Brent. <u>The Vanishing Border: A Photographic
Journey Along Our Frontier with Mexico</u>. Photographs by
Paul Conklin. New York: Dodd, Mead & Company, 1987.
175 p. ISBN: 0-396-08900-3. $14.95. Gr. 7-12.

(See review under UNITED STATES.)

*Bateman, Penny. <u>Aztecs and Incas: AD 1300-1532</u>. Illus-
trated by Rob Shone. New York: Franklin Watts, 1988.
32 p. ISBN: 0-531-10622-5. $11.90. Gr. 4-7.

This is definitely a well-designed overview of the Aztec
and Inca civilizations for young readers. By successfully
intermixing photographs, maps and colorful drawings with a

simple written text, this book provides highlights of these
civilizations in a most interesting manner. Students will
acquire an appreciation of the achievements, customs, homes,
religions, and other aspects of the Aztecs and Incas without feeling overwhelmed with too many facts or incidental
information.

Berdan, Frances F. The Aztecs. (Indians of North America)
New York: Chelsea House Publishers, 1989. 110 p.
ISBN: 1-55546-692-3. $16.95. Gr. 6-10.

The history of the Aztecs from the Olmecs until the Spanish Conquest is narrated in this attractive publication.
Numerous black-and-white graphics on almost every page
as well as a ten-page, full-color insert of the art of the
Aztec empire make this a useful introduction to Aztec culture.

*Berler, Beatrice. The Conquest of Mexico: A Modern Render-
ing of William H. Prescott's History. San Antonio, TX:
Corona Publishing Company, 1988. 143 p. ISBN: 0-931722-
69-1. $16.50. Gr. 8-adult.

Prescott's classic, History of the Conquest of Mexico, is
now available in this shortened version, which will definitely
appeal to readers not eager to undertake the original version. Berler has maintained the excitement of Prescott's
narrative by omitting minor episodes as well as Prescott's
philosophical discourses in this readable adaptation. All
of the well-known episodes of Cortés' incredible conquest of
Mexico are maintained, such as Cortés' first meeting with the
Tlaxcalans, Narváez insurrection, Montezuma's death, the
"Noche Triste" and other events. Modern readers should
realize, however, that this narrative reflects Prescott's
one-sided views regarding what he believed were "the ig-
norant, barbarian, savage natives" and "the civilized,
Christian Spaniards" and their "courageous, heroic leader,
Cortés." Throughout the narrative, the reader is exposed
to the faults of the Aztecs (for example, "New monarchs
were installed in regal dignity after their victorious campaign
netted a sufficient number of captives to serve as victims
for the bloody rites which stained the Aztec superstition,"
p. 6). About Montezuma, he states: "His pusillanimity

sprang from his superstition, as that superstition in the
savage is the substitute for religious principle in the civilized man" (p. 81). All of this is constantly contrasted
with Cortés "courage, valor and intelligence."

*Bierhorst, John. The Mythology of Mexico and Central Amer-
ica. New York: William Morrow and Company, Inc., 1990.
239 p. ISBN: 0-688-06721-2. $14.95. Gr. 9-adult.

As stated by the author in the introduction, this book is
"concerned with the stories that are heard at night, the
tales not told for mere entertainment, the ones that are
ancient, true, exemplary, filled with words of wisdom"
(p. 2). So, in these readable translations of twenty "basic
myths" readers/listeners will learn about the beginnings,
destructions, quest for corn, sun myths, journeys to the
other world as well as the storytellers of Mexico and
Central America. This is one of the best comprehensive
guides to the mythology of this region which will appeal to
either the scholar or the lover of pre-Columbian myths.

*Calderwood, Michael, and Gabriel Breña. Mexico, a Higher
Vision: An Aerial Journey from Past to Present. Photographs by Michael Calderwood. La Jolla, CA: Alti Publishing, 1990. 192 p. ISBN: 0-9625399-5-3. $49.95.
Gr. 6-Adult.

Spectacular, large-format publication that shows the beauty
and diversity of the Mexican landscape in some of the best
color photographs of Mexico ever published. The book is
organized by geographical areas--the southeast, the gulf
coast, the central plateau, etc.--with an excellent brief
introduction to each region which highlights its history, environment and special characteristics. This is indeed a
superior vision of Mexico that will appeal to the neophyte
or sophisticated reader. The only unappealing aspect of
this book is the prologue by Carlos Fuentes. This meta-
physical view of Mexican cosmogony may, unfortunately,
deter some readers from enjoying this otherwise wonderful
book.

Camp, Roderic A. Memoirs of a Mexican Politician. Illustrated

by Lawrence Mills. Albuquerque: University of New
Mexico Press, 1988. 230 p. ISBN: 0-8263-1042-7.
$11.95. Gr. 9-adult.

The author, who lived in Mexico City for a year when he
was nineteen years old and is now a professor of political
science in Pella, Iowa, wrote this fictionalized biography
of a Mexican politician because he believes that "there is
a scarcity of materials in English, from a Latin American
viewpoint, that deal with political life" (p. ix). Thus, he
combined his "first-hand knowledge of Mexican political life"
as told to him by politicians or as revealed in their memoirs.
There is no question that readers can learn something about
the political system in Mexico in this fictionalized memoir,
but what this novel lacks are genuine, human characters,
and a believable story. The following are examples of the
contrived thoughts and dialogues of the characters: "We
had very few material goods in those days. I sincerely
believe that I am not romanticizing my poor childhood, but
we did not have a strong desire for the consumer products
that overflow the shelves of urban department stores today" (p. 19). And this is how President López Mateos sup-
posedly addressed his "team" at a meeting in his private
office: "I don't care how many mistresses you have, or
what time you come to your office, that is your business,
but I want those obligations carried out, however best you
can achieve them" (pp. 200-201). There are many wonderful novels about life in Mexico, but this is not one of
them.

*Castellanos, Rosario. Another Way to Be: Selected Works
of Rosario Castellanos. Edited and translated by Myralyn
F. Allgood. Athens: The University of Georgia Press,
1990. 146 p. ISBN: 0-8203-1222-3. $25.00; ISBN: 0-
8203-1240-1. pap. $12.95. Gr. 9-adult.

A representative selection of Rosario Castellanos' literary
works is included in this well-prepared collection. Unfortunately, only fourteen of her poems include the original
Spanish version along with the English translation. The
poems in the introduction are represented in English translation only. In addition, it includes translations of four

short stories, excerpts from two of her best-known novels,
Balún-Canán and Oficio de Tinieblas, and six essays on
various topics. Readers unfamiliar with the life and works
of one of Mexico's most respected authors will find this
collection interesting and enjoyable, especially because this
is the only work available in English of Castellanos' work.

Catalano, Julie. The Mexican Americans. (The Peoples of
North America) New York: Chelsea House Publishers,
1988. 95 p. ISBN: 0-87754-857-9. $16.95. Gr. 4-8.

(See review under UNITED STATES.)

*Civilizations of the Americas. (History of the World) Mil-
waukee: Raintree Publishers, 1989. 80 p. ISBN: 0-8172-
3306-7. $15.50. Gr. 4-6.

(See review under LATIN AMERICA.)

*Clarke, Asa Bement. Travels in Mexico and California: Com-
prising a Journal of a Tour from Brazos Santiago, Through
Central Mexico, by Way of Monterrey, Chihuahua, the
Country of the Apaches, and the River Gila to the Mining
Districts of California. Edited by A. B. Clarke. College
Station: Texas A & M University Press, 1988. 143 p.
ISBN: 0-89096-354-1. $17.50. Gr. 8-adult.

A. B. Clarke, an adventurous former school teacher and
drugstore owner, describes his journey in 1849 from Massa-
chusetts to California through Mexico in a most exciting
daily journal. He presents detailed personal observations
of the country's physical environment as well as the lifestyles
and economic conditions of the Mexican Apache and Pima
peoples. His daily records reveal the harsh living conditions of those who traveled west during the Gold Rush.
In a candid and forthright manner, he tells about the
hunger, death from cholera, lack of water and other
deprivations that many endured. This is a wonderful exposure to the settling of the West through the eyes and
thoughts of one who did it.

Cooke, John Byrne. South of the Border. New York: Bantam Books, 1989. 324 p. ISBN: 0-553-05344-2. $17.95. Gr. 9-adult.

Lovers of westerns will enjoy this historical novel set in Mexico during the time of the Mexican Revolution. Flamboyant characters, such as Butch Cassidy and the well-known Mexican revolutionary Pancho Villa, add a sense of excitement to the novel's adventure and romance. The author must be commended for portraying this difficult era of U.S.-Mexico relations with great tact. He touches on controversial people and issues without seriously offending Mexican or American people.

Davis, James E., and Sharryl Davis Hawke. Mexico City. Milwaukee: Raintree Publishers, 1990. 64 p. ISBN: 0-8172-3029-7. $18.00. Gr. 4-7.

Through this focus on Mexico City, readers are supposed to learn about Mexican civilization. Hence, it explores Mexico City's history, cultural heritage, demographics, geography, and economic and natural resources. Superficially and from a tourist point of view, it may serve a purpose. But, unfortunately, this book is full of simplistic generalizations and absurd assertions as it emphasizes the problems of Mexico City. For example, describing the problems of sewage and garbage disposal, it states: "Collectors don't like to pick up garbage in the city's poor sections because people there don't throw away anything of value" (p. 30). Mexico City's sophistication and vitality are certainly missing while readers get a heavy dose, with appropriate photographs, of the pollution, poverty, unemployment and other problems of the city. There are misspelled or misused words throughout.

Desmond, Lawrence Gustave, and Phyllis Mauch Messenger. A Dream of Maya: Augustus and Alice Le Plongeon in

Nineteenth-Century Yucatan. Albuquerque: University
of New Mexico Press, 1988. 147 p. ISBN: 0-8263-1000-1.
$19.95. Gr. 9-adult.

The authors' purpose in writing this book was "to syn-
thesize the life of one of the most notable archaeologist-
travelers of the end of the nineteenth century and to let
the reader in on a number of previously unknown details
of his life" (p. xiv). Readers interested in Mayan culture
will be fascinated by the life of this controversial
archaeologist-photographer and his wife, Alice, who went
to Yucatán in 1873 to explore, to photograph and to prove
his hypothesis that "the Maya were founders of Egyptian
civilization." Even though the Le Plongeons' theories have
never been taken seriously, many do give them credit for
their contributions to the study of the Mayas through their
photographic documentation, descriptions and drawings.
This account gives them credit for their work and tries to
explain his problems with the established scholars of his
time. Numerous black-and-white photographs provide an
exciting view of the Mayan ruins and of the difficult cir-
cumstances in which this couple lived and worked.

*Diaz del Castillo, Bernal. Cortez and the Conquest of Mexi-
co by the Spaniards in 1521. Edited by B. G. Herzog.
Handen, CT: Linnet Books, 1988. 165 p. ISBN: 0-208-
02221-X. $17.50. Gr. 8-12.

This is an abridged edition of the excellent True History
of the Conquest of New Spain by Bernal Diaz del Castillo,
one of the soldiers who accompanied Cortez. It is illustrated with black-and-white drawings by sixteenth-century
Indian artists employed by Fra Sahagun, a Franciscan priest.
The excitement and incredible adventures that resulted in
the conquest of Mexico by a small group of Spaniards is
recorded in one of the best historical narratives ever
written. This abridged version should interest the most
indifferent student of the history of Mexico.

Fisher, Leonard Everett. Pyramid of the Sun, Pyramid of
the Moon. New York: Macmillan Publishing Company, 1988.
[32 p.] ISBN: 0-02-735300-1. $13.95. Gr. 4-6.

Spectacular two-page gray illustrations of the pyramids of
the Sun and Moon in Teotihuacan, Mexico, convey to the
reader some of the majesty of these pre-Columbian pyramids. Unfortunately, the brief narrative confuses the
reader by trying to include the history of the pyramids
and the Aztecs in a few pages when in fact the two civilizations were separated by more than one thousand years.
Also disturbing is the author/illustrator's compulsion to
emphasize the Aztec practice of human sacrifice--both in a
dramatic illustration and the text: "... To keep the gods
happy, the Aztecs took enemy warriors alive and tore their
beating hearts from their chests on the stone altar of the
Great Temple Pyramid..." and on and on. Readers should
realize that this Temple is not near the pyramids--it is
part of a different civilization and in a different location
in Mexico. One good photograph of the pyramids of the
Sun and Moon would accomplish what this book ostensibly
tries to do.

Fuentes, Carlos. Myself with Others: Selected Essays.
New York: Farrar, Straus & Giroux, 1988. 214 p. ISBN:
0-374-21750-5. $19.95. Gr. 9-adult.

Carlos Fuentes, a well-known Mexican writer, expounds on
his own writing, his political beliefs and his opinion of
such other writers as Cervantes, Diderot, Gogol, Borges,
Kundera and García Márquez, as well as Luis Buñuel and
the "cinema of freedom," in this collection of previously
published essays. Admirers of this author will be impressed
others will know what to expect.

*George, Jean Craighead. Shark Beneath the Reef. New
York: Harper & Row, Publishers, 1989. 182 p. ISBN:
0-06-021992-0. $11.89. Gr. 6-9.

Tomás, a fourteen-year-old Mexican boy, is determined to
catch a shark, the greatest prize for the fishermen of the
Sea of Cortez. When he finally does so, he realizes that
life is much more complex than being a hero in his home
town. He still must make an important decision--should he
go to school or become a fisherman. By combining interesting aspects of Mexico's pre-Columbian and modern history, as well as sad realities of contemporary Mexico (such

as the abuse of government officials), with the personal
dilemmas of an adolescent boy about his future, the author
has created an exciting coming-of-age story with a Mexican
flavor. There are a few unnecessary generalizations that,
perhaps, are a result of the author's own lack of knowledge
or misunderstandings of Mexican people and customs. For
example: "The three fishermen jumped out and smiled to a
group of unemployed men who were idling away time on the
beach. They gathered around to watch the Tórreses un-
load. Watching is a national pastime in Mexico and only
occasionally does someone step forward to help" (p. 39).

Gleiter, Jan. Benito Juárez.
Thompson, Kathleen. Sor Juana Inés de la Cruz.
    Ea. vol.: 32 p. (Raintree Hispanic Stories) Milwaukee:
    Raintree Publishers, 1990. $15.33. Gr. 3-5.

    (See review under SPAIN: Codye, Corinn....)

Gleiter, Jan, and Kathleen Thompson. David Farragut. Il-
    lustrated by Francis Balistreri. ISBN: 0-8172-2904-3.
    _____. Diego Rivera. Illustrated by Yoshi Miyake. ISBN:
    0-8172-2908-6.
    _____. Junípero Serra. Illustrated by Charles Shaw.
    ISBN: 0-8172-2909-4.
    Ea. vol.: 32 p. Milwaukee: Raintree Publishers, 1989.
    $15.99. Gr. 3-5.

The lives of three notable Hispanics from Mexico, the
United States and Spain are briefly narrated in these bilingual (Spanish/English) books. Even though there is
nothing particularly exciting about these titles, they do
provide basic facts about the lives and accomplishments
of these three Hispanic men who excelled in the U.S. Civil
War, in the arts and in the development of missions in
California. Unfortunately, these social studies books will
remind many readers of their textbooks, especially the
bland watercolor illustrations and the lackluster Spanish and
English texts. The content, however, is inspiring and
true.

Gomez, Paolo. Food in Mexico. (International Food Library)

Vero Beach, FL: Rourke Publications, Inc., 1989. 32 p.
ISBN: 0-86625-341-6. $9.50. Gr. 6-adult.

This is a superficial introduction to Mexican food products,
regional dishes and cooking techniques, including a few
recipes. The best part of the book is the few pages that
briefly describe agriculture in Mexico. Otherwise, it is a
most disappointing view of Mexico with stereotypical photos
of poor barefooted children, Mexican "mariachis," poor people at an outdoor market with the incredible statement:
"Most Mexicans prefer to shop at markets like this 'tiangui'"
(p. 10) and other tourist-type observations and photos.
To top it off, the following words in Spanish are misspelled:
"Guatamala" [sic] (p. 6), "tostados" [sic] (p. 13), "Cortès"
[sic] (p. 14), and "mole Poblana" [sic] (p. 16). There is
definitely much more to "food in Mexico" than what this
book portrays.

Hall, Douglas Kent. The Border: Life on the Line. New
York: Abbeville Press Publishers, 1988. 251 p. ISBN:
0-89659-685-0. $35.00. Gr. 9-adult.

In a spirited and most personal manner, Hall writes about
life in both sides of the U.S.-Mexico border. Like most
books on the same topic, the author/photographer chose to
dwell on the negative aspects of life in that region: "Crossing the bridge over the Rio Grande ... was like a leap into
a dark and sinister dream. It brought back every story I
had ever heard about Mexico. I had been warned about the
food, about the water, about pickpockets and bandits, about
whores and disease, about the terrible treachery of Mexicans in general" (p. 13). Hence, it is not surprising that
he found, photographed and interviewed an incredible number of people who "are starving to death in Mexico" as well
as the usual smugglers, refugees, illegal aliens and prostitutes. He also met a priest, a kindly agent, and some
dedicated ranchers, artists and teachers. Numerous black-
and-white and color photographs add a certain poignancy
to the narrative, but with two exceptions, they depict the
life of the very poor. This is a compelling testimony to
the sordid aspects of life on the border. One wonders why
no one bothered to check the Spanish words used in the
book--most are misspelled or misused.

*Hall, Linda B., and Don M. Coerver. Revolution on the
Border: The United States and Mexico, 1910-1920. Albuquerque: The University of New Mexico Press, 1988.
205 p. ISBN: 0-8263-1234-9. pap. $14.95. Gr. 9-adult.

(See review under UNITED STATES.)

*Haskins, Jim. Count Your Way Through Mexico. Illustrated
by Helen Byers. Minneapolis: Carolrhoda Books, Inc.,
1989. [22 p.] ISBN: 0-87614-349-4. $10.95. Gr. 4-7.

Through the numbers one to ten in Spanish, the author
introduces various concepts about Mexico and its culture.
This is an imaginative way to expose young readers to basic
aspects of the history, folklore, arts, foods and animals
of Mexico. The soft pencil illustrations in color and the
simple text provide enough information without overwhelming young readers.

Hunter, Nigel. The Expeditions of Cortés. Illustrated by
Peter Bull. (Great Journeys) New York: The Book-
wright Press, 1990. 32 p. ISBN: 0-531-18355-1. $11.40.
Gr. 5-8.

This is a sensationalized account of Cortés' life as an adventurer which culminates in his conquest and domination
of the Aztec civilization in Mexico. Neither the extrava-
gant watercolor illustrations nor the flimsy narrative do
justice to the Aztecs or to Hernán Cortés. The Aztecs are
portrayed as blood-starved savages and Cortés as a dis-
satisfied "conquistador."

*James, Ian. Inside Mexico. New York: Franklin Watts,
1989. 32 p. ISBN: 0-531-10761-2. $11.40. Gr. 4-8.

This is an excellent, up-to-date introduction to the land,
history, people, arts, economy, industry and other aspects
of Mexico. The simple and direct text and the numerous
outstanding photographs in color combine to make this one
of the best introductions to Mexico today.

*Juana Inés de la Cruz, Sister. A Sor Juana Anthology.
  Translated by Alan S. Trueblood. Cambridge, MA: Harvard University Press, 1988. 248 p. ISBN: 0-674-82120-3.
  $29.95. Gr. 10-adult.

This outstanding anthology includes bilingual (Spanish/
English) samples of the best poetry by Juana Inés de la
Cruz as well as excerpts (in English only) which demonstrate her skill as a writer of prose and poetic drama.
English-speaking readers should be exposed to Sor Juana
Inés de la Cruz, who is considered one of the finest Hispanic poets of the seventeenth century. This excellent
translation of her work makes this possible. Even though
this anthology was done to accompany Octavio Paz's superior
study, Sor Juana, young adult readers will find basic information on the life and work of this outstanding woman
in the Introduction. Few authors have expressed with such
passion and understanding "the right of women to pursue
lives of learning, to cultivate artistic gifts and to embrace
public careers" and to read this from a nun who wrote in
a Catholic convent in the seventeenth century in New
Spain is indeed remarkable and inspiring.

Langley, Lester D. MexAmerica: Two Countries, One Future.

(See review under UNITED STATES.)

Lattimore, Deborah Nourse. The Flame of Peace: A Tale of
  the Aztecs. Illustrated by the author. New York:
  Harper and Row, Publishers, 1987. 40 p. ISBN: 0-06-
  023708-2. $12.95. Gr. 4-6.

The author and illustrator has combined Aztec mythology,
art and her own imagination to produce this story about
a brave Aztec boy, Two Flint, who brought peace to his
people. The magnificent illustrations are the best part
of this book. On parchment-like paper, the red-bordered
artwork is most reminiscent of Aztec codices. The illustrations exude the joy and vigor of Aztec life. The story,
however, is confusing and long-winded.

Lattimore, Deborah Nourse. Why There Is No Arguing in

Heaven: A Mayan Myth. New York: Harper & Row, Publishers, 1989. [32 p.] ISBN: 0-06-023717-1. $13.89.
Gr. 4-7.

By combining different interpretations, the author/illustrator
has created a new version of the Mayan creation story. The
most noteworthy aspect of this publication are the stunning
watercolor illustrations which convey the spirit of the Maya
through sensitive reproduction of their ruins and sculptures.
Some teachers might like to use this myth with students in
grades 4 through 7 as a background to the study of Mayan
religion.

*Long, Jeff. Duel of Eagles: The Mexican and U.S. Fight
for the Alamo. New York: William Morrow and Company,
1990. 431 p. ISBN: 0-688-07252-6. $22.95. Gr. 9-
adult.

(See review under UNITED STATES.)

Martínez, Oscar J. Troublesome Border. Tucson: University of Arizona Press, 1988. 177 p. ISBN: 0-8165-1033-4.
$22.95. Gr. 9-adult.

(See review under UNITED STATES.)

*Moran, Tom. A Family in Mexico. Minneapolis: Lerner
Publications Company, 1987. 32 p. ISBN: 0-8225-1677-2.
$8.95. Gr. 3-6.

Attractive photographs in color and a simple text tell about
Paula María Fosado, a nine-year-old girl who lives in the
state of Oaxaca in southwestern Mexico. Through her daily
activities, readers will learn basic facts and interesting customs of the people who live in a small city in Mexico. The
most valuable aspect of this publication is that it includes
a realistic balance of photographs of a nice middle-class
family and poor rural scenes.

Morey, Janet, and Wendy Dunn. Famous Mexican Americans.
New York: E. P. Dutton, 1989. 176 p. ISBN: 0-525-
65012-1. $14.95. Gr. 6-9.

The life and accomplishments of fourteen Mexican American men and women are briefly recounted in this collection
of biographical sketches. Each life story traces the roots
of the individual's achievement and relates childhood memories, current information and special beliefs. Black-and-
white photographs illustrate each essay; unfortunately,
some are blurred and unclear. The biographees are Cesar
Chavez, Henry Cisneros, Patrick Flores, Dolores Huerta,
Nancy Lopez, Vilma Martinez, Luis Nogales, Edward James
Olmos, Katherine Davalos Ortega, Blandina Cardenas Ramirez
Edward R. Roybal, Dan Sosa Jr., Luis Valdez and William
Velasquez.

Ochoa, George. The Fall of Mexico City. (Turning Points
   in American History) Englewood Cliffs, NJ: Silver Burdett Press, 1989. 64 p. ISBN: 0-381-09836-6. Gr. 5-8.

Through numerous black-and-white and color photographs
and maps and a simple narrative, young readers are introduced to the Mexican-American War. As explained by the
author: "The story of the Mexican War is a story of fierce
battle, political intrigue, and the popular dream of 'manifest destiny'--America's belief that it was destined by God
to spread across the continent. It is also the story of a
moral debate on the use of American power that is still
going on today" (p. 9). In many ways this book will remind readers of their history textbooks: many facts are
presented, and many important and unimportant issues are
discussed in the same "balanced" manner. The result is a
bland narrative that will not spark much interest. Some
historians will question the author's conclusion: "Perhaps
the most lasting issue raised by the Mexican War is in the
area of foreign relations. The war marked a new readiness
on the part of the United States to send its armed forces
abroad.... Since the Mexican War, the United States has
intervened in many parts of Latin America for many different reasons" (p. 57).

Odijk, Pamela. The Aztecs. (The Ancient World) Englewood
   Cliffs, NJ: Silver Burdett Press, 1990. 47 p. ISBN:
   0-382-09887-0. $14.98. Gr. 4-7.

It is indeed unfortunate that the beautiful design of this

book--including excellent photographs in color, pleasant
layout and good-quality paper--is not matched by an engaging or interesting narrative. Numerous facts are presented in a monotonous, uninspiring manner as the author
surveys the culture, government, religion, and wars of the
Aztecs. This book may be useful as a basic introduction
to the Aztecs, but readers will never comprehend the marvelous achievements of the Aztecs. For example, the following is the only reference to the great Aztec sculptures,
which have amazed historians and artists for centuries:
"Sculptures which have survived include the status of the
goddess, Coatlicue, the stone of Tizoc, and the Calendar
Stone, which was the largest known Aztec carving" (p.
34). And, despite numerous photographs, it includes none
of this most important Aztec achievement.

Oster, Patrick. The Mexicans: A Personal Portrait of a
People. New York: William Morrow and Company, Inc.,
1989. 334 p. ISBN: 0-688-08193-2. $19.95. Gr. 9-adult.

The author states in the introduction that Mexicans are as
different from Americans as "a chili pepper is from apple
pie." So, to help Americans understand the people of
Mexico, he wrote this collection of twenty stories about
mostly poor Mexicans and added numerous statistics regarding Mexico's problems of "poverty, illiteracy, income dispar-
ity, unemployment, malnutrition, crime, political repression,
smuggling, massive foreign debt, bulging budget deficits,
horrific environmental conditions, rural violence, corruption,
religious fanaticism, racism, and weaknesses of the character"
(p. 286). This is indeed a readable human and factual
compendium of the many serious problems of Mexico in the
1980s. Unfortunately, it does not offer any hint of the
many wonderful and positive aspects of Mexico. Readers
will find very little that they can respect or admire in their
neighbors to the south in this dismal portrait of Mexican
people.

Paulsen, Gary. The Crossing. New York: Orchard Books,
Franklin Watts, Inc., 1987. 114 p. ISBN: 0-531-05709-8.
$11.95. Gr. 7-10.

Manuel, a fourteen-year-old poor Mexican boy, has always

lived on the streets of Juárez, Mexico, across from El
Paso, Texas. There he meets Robert S. Locke, an American sergeant and Vietnam veteran who, despite being a
perfect officer, needs to get completely drunk every night.
Their difficult personal problems are set against a superficial view of Mexico with the customary "frijoles," "tortillas"
and bullfights. Reluctant readers might be encouraged by
the simple writing style and brevity of this novel, but
most readers will be turned off by the insurmountable problems of an orphan boy who had no one in this world and
by the shallow characterization of an American vet. In
addition, it is distressing to read one more novel that
deals only with the worst aspects of a Mexican border town--
violence, poverty, prostitution and human abuse.

*Paz, Octavio. The Collected Poems of Octavio Paz, 1957-
1987. Edited and translated by Eliot Weinberger. New
York: New Directions, W. W. Norton & Co., Inc., 1987.
669 p. ISBN: 0-8112-1037-5. $37.50. Gr. 10-adult.

This remarkable bilingual (Spanish-English) edition includes
all the poetry published by Octavio Paz in book form since
1957. More than half of the nearly two hundred poems
have never appeared before in an English-language edition.
Sophisticated Spanish-speaking poetry lovers will delight in
Octavio Paz's strength and sensibility; English readers will
be moved by the touching translations. This is definitely
a superior collection of Octavio Paz's poems (Paz was the
1990 Nobel laureate in literature.)

*Paz, Octavio. Sor Juana. Translated by Margaret Sayers
Peden. Cambridge, MA: Harvard University Press, 1988.
547 p. ISBN: 0-674-82105-X. $29.95. Gr. 10-adult.

The life and times of Sor Juana Inés de la Cruz, the most
important writer of New Spain of the seventeenth century,
are narrated by Mexico's leading poet in this engrossing
biography. Readers will be fascinated not only by the
incredible life of this great poet but by Paz's extraordinary
historical analysis of New Spain during colonial times. The
following is an example of the author's ability to write literary criticism in its true historical context. Regarding
the well-known "redondilla" in which Sor Juana censures

men and defends women, Paz states: "In this sense, the
poem was a historical watershed, a beginning: for the
first time in the history of our literature a woman is speaking in her own name, defending her sex and, with grace
and intelligence, using the same weapons as the detractors
of her sex, accusing them of the very vices they impute
to women.... It is even more noteworthy that this satire
should have been written in New Spain, a closed, peripheral
society under two zealot powers, the Catholic Church and
the Spanish monarchy" (p. 304). Serious students of the
viceroyalty of New Spain as well as poetry lovers will be
moved and intrigued by the life and work of this brave
woman as depicted by Octavio Paz.

*Porter, Elliot, and Ellen Auerbach. Mexican Churches. Al-
buquerque: University of New Mexico Press, 1987.
[109 p.] ISBN: 0-8263-1023-0. $24.95. Gr. 10-adult.

In the fall of 1955 the authors went on a photo excursion
to Mexico. Their "only goal was to get pictures which show
the saints and their surroundings as they are revered by
the Mexican people" (p. 7). The results are eight excellent photo plates in color of mostly interiors of churches
all over Mexico. The superior quality of these photographs
and the well-written introduction by Donna Pierce provide
the reader with an intimate view of the religious beliefs
and shared traditions of the people of Mexico.

*Ragan, John David. Emiliano Zapata. (World Leaders Past
& Present) New York: Chelsea House Publishers, 1989.
111 p. ISBN: 1-55546-823-3. $16.95. Gr. 7-12.

Through the life and times of Emiliano Zapata, readers are
exposed to the Mexican Revolution, the first of the great
revolutions of the twentieth century. Like other biographies
in this series, it is heavily illustrated with outstanding black-
and-white photos of the period. In addition, the author's
objectivity in presenting difficult issues of this turbulent
era in Mexico's history makes this one of the best introductions for adolescents to some of Mexico's most controversial
leaders, such as Porfirio Diaz, Francisco Madero, Pancho
Villa, and Victoriano Huerta. Few will disagree with the
author's description of Emiliano Zapata: "Unlike so many

people fighting for power in Mexico at that time, he could not be bought and would not compromise on the one demand that meant everything to his followers: land reform. In this quiet man the villagers of Morelos had found a skillful and charismatic leader of great personal integrity, who inspired an almost religious devotion in the state's agricultural population" (p. 33).

*Rohmer, Harriet, and Mary Anchondo. How We Came to the Fifth World/Cómo vinimos al quinto mundo: A Creation Story from Ancient Mexico.

(See Review under PUERTO RICO.)

Schele, Linda, and David Freidel. A Forest of Kings: The Untold Story of the Ancient Maya. Photographs by Justin Kerr. New York: William Morrow and Company, 1990. 542 p. ISBN: 0-688-07456-1. $29.95. Gr. 10-adult.

The authors--two experts on Maya writing, art and archeology--have combined their interests to present a history of the Maya. They state that this Maya history is "a construction of our times, sensibilities, and intellectual agendas" (p. 403). Hence, this personalized story of Maya kingship, from the beginning of its institution and the first great pyramid builders two thousand years ago to the decline of Maya civilization, will be of special interest to serious students of the ancient Maya. Numerous black-and-white drawings, maps and charts on almost every page add further to the authors' detailed narrative.

Shetterly, Susan Hand. The Dwarf-Wizard of Uxmal. Illustrated by Robert Shetterly. New York: Macmillan Publishing Company, 1990. [30 p.] ISBN: 0-689-31455-8. $13.95. Gr. 2-4.

The Mayan legend about Tol, the dwarf-wizard who became the ruler of the city of Uxmal and the leader of his people, is retold in a fast-moving, exciting narrative, which has maintained many authentic Mayan symbols, food and ceremonies. However, the colorful illustrations are grotesque caricatures of Mayan people and culture without the refineme elegance and beauty of the Mayan culture of the Yucatan peninsula. The illustrations are sad misinterpretations of one of the greatest pre-Columbian cultures. As such, they are only negative stereotypes of the Mayan civilization.

Steel, Anne. An Aztec Warrior. Illustrated by John James. (How They Lived) Vero Beach, FL: Rourke Enterprises, Inc., 1988. 32 p. ISBN: 0-86592-146-6. $12.67. Gr. 3-6.

The visuals are the best part of this title that tells about the life of an Aztec warrior. The richly textured illustrations are complemented with excellent small photographs in color, which convey the lifestyle, social order, battles, religion, and other aspects of Aztec society. This is, however, a very one-sided introduction to Aztec civilization. Of course, it devotes several pages to the Aztec practice of human sacrifice in all its gory detail, for example: "The victims were killed on stone slabs at the very top of the temple. The priests tore out their hearts and offered them up to the gods. These priests were a terrifying sight. They wore black or green cloaks embroidered with human skulls, and their bodies were covered with black paint. They never washed their long hair, but left it matted with blood" (p. 18). And, incredibly, it doesn't even mention one of the greatest Aztec achievements--their marvelous sculptures and other artistic creations. This is certainly not the way to introduce young people to Aztec civilization.

*Street-Porter, Tim. Casa Mexicana. Photographs by the author. New York: Stewart, Tabori and Chang, 1989. 272 p. ISBN: 1-55670-097-0. $50.00. Gr. 8-adult.

The beauty and variety of Mexican houses are exquisitely depicted in this handsome large-format publication with over 350 photographs in color and a readable and informative text. The excellent design and arrangement provide readers with an appealing introduction to Mexican architecture and interior design, including an in-depth view of Mexican haciendas, homes of artists, the genius of Luis Barragán and other aspects of Mexican art and design.

*Weintraub, Sidney. A Marriage of Convenience: Relations Between Mexico and the United States. New York: Oxford University Press, 1990. 270 p. ISBN: 0-19-506125-X. $24.95. Gr. 10-adult.

Sidney Weintraub, who has held several positions at the U.S. State Department and is currently Dean Rusk Professor at the Lyndon B. Johnson School of Public Affairs at the University of Texas, is the author of this remarkable analysis of the relationship between Mexico and the United States. In a most objective and incisive manner, he describes crucial issues that affect the interlocked destinies of both countries as well as policy issues in such important matters as trade, industry, energy, debt, the border and migration. It is indeed refreshing to read about serious problems between Mexico and the U.S. depicted with much honesty and frankness. For example, in discussing "the problem of corruption," Weintraub states, "... it remains most indelicate for a non-Mexican to pronounce on Mexican corruption" (p. 58) and yet he proceeds to discuss it in a forthright manner. Weintraub also displays his usual candor in his conclusions and recommendations: He states: "Mexico ... does not abet a cooperative relationship by continuing to believe that it can obtain economic concessions even as it constantly lambasts the United States at home and in foreign-policy forums.... The United States will not be seen as a friend if it continues to approach relations with Mexico in a condescending way ..." (p. 206). It is difficult to find a more open account of U.S.-Mexico relations without the customary political diatribes or diplomatic half-truths.

*Zamora, Martha. Frida Kahlo: The Brush of Anguish. Abridged and translated by Marilyn Sode Smith. San Francisco: Chronicle Books, 1990. 143 p. ISBN: 0-87701-746-8. $29.95. Gr. 10-adult.

The life and work of Frida Kahlo, one of Mexico's highly renowned painters, are depicted in this lavishly illustrated, large-format publication. It includes seventy-five color reproductions of her paintings, as well as numerous photographs that reveal the personal joys and sorrows of the famous artist and wife of Diego Rivera. The well-done and sensitive translation/abridgment will satisfy the most ardent admirer of this long-suffering artist.

NICARAGUA

Angel, Adriana, and Fiona Macintosh. The Tiger's Milk: Women of Nicaragua. New York: Henry Holt and Company, 1987. 142 p. ISBN: 0-8050-0638-9. $18.95. Gr. 9-adult.

The hardships and tragic lives of poor women in Nicaragua are movingly depicted in these testimonies which describe life in the Atlantic and Pacific coasts of this Central American country. Through excellent black-and-white photographs and stirring personal accounts, readers will sympathize with the abuses that many generations of Nicaraguan women have had to endure. Despite the fact that there is an overdose of anti-U.S. feelings in the introduction written by Hermione Harris and the authors' preface, women everywhere will empathize with Nicaraguan women who have had to struggle against machismo and poverty. This is what makes this book so special.

Cummins, Ronnie. Nicaragua. (Children of the World) Photographs by Rose Welch. Milwaukee: Gareth-Stevens Children's Books, 1990. 64 p. ISBN: 0-8368-0221-7. $12.95. Gr. 3-5.

Ten-year-old Michael Eduardo lives with his mother, grandparents, aunts, uncles, and cousins in San Jerónimo, a neighborhood in León, Nicaragua's second largest city. Through attractive photographs in color and a simple text, readers are introduced to Michael Eduardo's life at home, at school and with his family and friends. Like other titles in this series, it includes fifteen pages of information about Nicaragua's history, government, natural

resources, culture, and currency as well as suggestions
for research projects and other activities.

*DeSauza, James. Brother Anansi and the Cattle Ranch/El
hermano Anansi y el rancho de ganado. Illustrated by
Stephen Von Mason. Adapted by Harriet Rohmer. Spanish
version: Rosalma Zubizarreta. San Francisco: Children's
Book Press, 1989. 32 p. ISBN: 0-89239-044-1. $12.95.
Gr. 3-6.

In a lighthearted and amusing manner, this outstanding
bilingual (English/Spanish) adaptation of a Nicaraguan tale
shows how Anansi outwits Tiger and ends up with all the
cattle from their cattle-raising business. Children will enjoy reading about Anansi's resourcefulness and looking at
the striking, full-page, colorful illustrations which perfectly convey the joyful mood of this tale.

Gelman, Rita Golden. Inside Nicaragua: Young People's
Dreams and Fears. New York: Franklin Watts, 1988.
189 p. ISBN: 0-531-15085-2. $13.00. Gr. 8-12.

In a passionate and intense manner, the author describes
her experiences traveling through Nicaragua. She states:
"I have come to Nicaragua to see for myself who the real
villains are and to write a book about young people here,
about what it's like to live in a country at war" (p. 18).
After a few months in which she observes the effects of
the present conflict on the lives of the young people of
Nicaragua she describes her "own feelings of anger about
the role the United States is playing in all of this" (p.
169). She reports that she has "seen no indications of
terrorism on the part of the Sandinistas" (p. 125). Gelman
quotes young Nicaraguans who state, "'Don't support your
government. Demonstrate against Reagan'" (p. 154).
This is obviously a pro-Sandinista, anti-Reagan view of
the problems in Nicaragua today.

Gutman, Roy. Banana Diplomacy: The Making of American
Policy in Nicaragua, 1981-1987. New York: Simon and
Schuster, 1988. 404 p. ISBN: 0-671-60626-3. $19.95.
Gr. 9-adult.

(See review under UNITED STATES.)

Jenkins, Tony. Nicaragua and the United States. New York:
    Franklin Watts, 1989. 190 p. ISBN: 0-531-10795-7.
    $14.90. Gr. 8-12.

In a strong anti-American tone, the author traces the history of the relationship between Nicaragua and the United
States from the nineteenth century up to the spring of
1989. In the beginning, the author explains the notorious
William Walker's attempts to become president of Nicaragua:
"To many Americans it seemed that theirs was a superior
civilization that had a right and a duty to continue expand-
ing throughout the Western Hemisphere, and Walker was
popular for the way in which he seemed to embody this
'manifest destiny' of the United States to conquer and
'civilize' all of the Americas" (p. 10). The following is
one of many explanations of how U.S. presidents have
dealt with Latin America: "Roosevelt was convinced that
'superior' nations had the right and the duty to dominate
'inferior' ones in the interests of civilization" (p. 24).
The author concludes by quoting Goodfellow: " 'Nicaragua
now stands as an example of what happens if you dare
defy Uncle Sam'" (p. 171). This is a diatribe against the
United States and an apology for the Sandinistas in Nicaragua. The book includes black-and-white photographs,
many of which are blurred and unclear.

*Lake, Anthony. Somoza Falling. Boston: Houghton Mifflin
    Company, 1989. 317 p. ISBN: 0-395-41983-2. $18.95.
    Gr. 9-adult.

In a direct and straightforward manner, the author, who
was director of policy planning in the State Department
during the Carter administration, describes how things
work within the world of foreign policy making. He carefully reconstructs Washington's reaction to the gathering
crisis in Nicaragua during 1978 and 1979, the end of the
regime of Anastasio Somoza. He explains that he chose this
case "because it represents a policy failure." Lake is concerned about the trend in the State Department that began
in the mid-1960s which trains and promotes generalists and
managers at the expense of area experts. He prefers a

balance between "the limiting caution of career officials
and the policy priorities of political appointees" (p. 29).
This is a most informative account of prerevolutionary
events in Nicaragua and the United States.

*Lye, Keith. Take a Trip to Nicaragua. (Take a Trip to)
New York: Franklin Watts, 1988. 32 p. ISBN: 0-531-
10559-8. $10.90. Gr. 2-4.

In a terse and concise manner, this appealing publication
introduces young readers to many aspects of the people
and country of Nicaragua. Clear, color photographs on
every page and a simple narrative provide quite a bit of
basic information about this Central American country without overwhelming children.

Rohmer, Harriet, adapter. Uncle Nicho's Hat/El sombrero
del tío Nacho. Illustrated by Veg Reisberg. Spanish version: Rosalma Zubizarreta. San Francisco: Children's
Book Press, 1989. 32 p. ISBN: 0-89239-043-3. $12.95.
Gr. 3-6.

Through this well-done bilingual adaption of a Nicaraguan
folktale, children are supposed to understand the difficulties of making changes and shaking off old habits. Perhaps
some children will be able to see the connection between
Uncle Nacho's old hat, which he tries to discard, and his
new hat, which is the voice of youthful change. Bold,
bright watercolor illustrations with a strong Latin American
flavor complement this tale.

Rohmer, Harriet, and Dorminster Wilson. Mother Scorpion
Country/La tierra de la Madre Escorpión. Illustrated by
Virginia Stearns. Spanish version: Rosalma Zubizarreta
and Alma Flor Ada. (Stories from Central America/Cuentos
de Centroamérica) San Francisco: Children's Book Press,
1987. 32 p. ISBN: 0-89239-032-8. $10.95. Gr. 3-6.

The love between a brave young Miskito Indian, Naklili,
and his young wife, Kati, is warmly depicted in this bilingual (English/Spanish) adaptation of a Nicaraguan tale.
Bold, colorful illustrations of Naklili following Kati from the

land of the living to the spirit world make this tale a
little more understandable to young readers.

Rohmer, Harriet; Octavio Chow; and Morris Vidaure. The
Invisible Hunters/Los cazadores invisibles. Illustrated by
Joe Sam. Spanish version: Rosalma Zubizarreta and Alma
Flor Ada. (Stories from Central America/Cuentos de
Centroamérica) San Francisco: Children's Book Press,
1987. 32 p. ISBN: 0-89239-031-X. $10.95. Gr. 3-6.

The impact of the first European traders on the life of the
Miskito Indians in the seventeenth century in Nicaragua is
retold in this bilingual (English/Spanish) legend. Colorful collage-style illustrations add a sense of rhythm and
movement to this little-known Nicaraguan tale.

PANAMA

Briggs, Clarence E. Operation Just Cause: Panama Decem-
ber 1989, a Soldier's Eyewitness Account. Harrisburg,
PA: Stackpole Books, 1990. 155 p. ISBN: 0-8117-
2520-0. pap. $10.95. Gr. 9-adult.

This personal account by a rifle company executive officer
who participated in U.S. operations in Panama in 1989 describes the rules of engagement, the preparation and
planning, the success of the operation, as well as the im-
plications for the future of similar engagements. It is
important to note that the author does not engage in philosophical or political issues regarding the invasion; rather,
he vividly depicts the military operation itself and the
problems of peacekeeping actions. Young adults interested
in a soldier's viewpoint regarding this military operation
will find this book illuminating and most readable.

Dolan, Edward F. Panama and the United States: Their
Canal. Their Stormy Years. New York: Franklin Watts,
1990. 160 p. ISBN: 0-531-10911-9. $13.90. Gr. 8-12.

This history of Panama's relations with the United States
includes the earliest dreams of an Atlantic-Pacific link.
Panama's independence with American help, the actual construction of the Canal and the strife between the two countries as a result of the Canal are discussed in a straightforward manner. Numerous black-and-white photos, drawings and maps add interest to this well-done narrative.
Perhaps some readers might question the author's assertions
regarding U.S. wrongs in Panama without giving considera-
tion to Panama's domestic problems and its own

73

inconsistencies. This is another example of how many U.S. authors discuss only U.S. wrongs in international affairs, disregarding wrongs committed by other countries.

*Oliver, Carl R. Panama's Canal. New York: Franklin Watts, 1990. 96 p. ISBN: 0-531-10958-5. $13.90. Gr. 6-12.

In a lively and forthright manner the author discusses the history of the Panama Canal, the technological, political and human problems that had to be overcome to build the canal, the current challenges and the many unanswered questions regarding the future of the canal. This is indeed a candid overview of the psychosocial, economic and political issues surrounding the Panama Canal. Excellent black-and-white historical and contemporary photographs add to the value of this book.

*St. George, Judith. The Panama Canal. New York: G. P. Putnam's Sons, 1989. 159 p. ISBN: 0-399-21637-5. $15.95. Gr. 7-12.

This is a comprehensive, informative and well-written account of the history, technical and scientific achievements of the Panama Canal, as well as the human drama behind its construction. By concentrating on the key personalities involved in the construction of the canal, the author adds a sense of history and great consequence to the canal itself. In addition, the author describes in a direct and clear manner the tremendous technical difficulties and social problems that had to be overcome before the canal was finally completed. Numerous black-and-white historical photos, maps and artwork add to the value and interest of this excellent publication.

Stewart, Gail B. Panama. (Places in the News) New York: Crestwood House, Macmillan Publishing Company, 1990. 48 p. ISBN: 0-89686-536-3. $10.95. Gr. 6-8.

The arrest of Panama's leader, Manuel Antonio Noriega, by the United States government is the focus for this examination of historical and recent events that have kept Panama in the news. Readers will be bored by most of this choppy,

monotonous narrative that relates the history of Panama
from the early sixteenth century up to 1983, when General
Noriega became the head of the National Guard. The last
ten pages, however, are more interesting and informative.
They provide a straightforward discussion of important issues "that troubled many U.S. government leaders" as well
as raise questions regarding the U.S. invasion of Panama
and the arrest of Noriega.

PARAGUAY

Haverstock, Nathan A. <u>Paraguay in Pictures</u>. (Visual Geography Series) Minneapolis: Lerner Publications Company, 1987. ISBN: 0-8225-1819-8. $9.95. Gr. 5-9.

The land, history, government, people and economy of
Paraguay are described through a most objective text and
numerous black-and-white and color photographs. This is
not a superficial overview of the small, landlocked country
in the heart of South America, but rather an insightful
discussion of the important issues surrounding Paraguay up
to 1986. For example, the following is Haverstock's accurate
description of Asunción, the capital: "Although the city
follows a Spanish design, with rectangular blocks laid out
around a central plaza, the plain, drab buildings reflect
the fact that Asunción is the chief city of a comparatively
poor country" (pp. 19-20). And, in discussing Alfredo
Stroessner's leadership, he states: "But although Paraguay
under Stroessner has experienced economic growth, only a
small group of wealthy Paraguayans has been affected by
the progress. Furthermore, the stability of Stroessner's
long rule has been at considerable cost to political rights
and individual freedoms" (p. 37).

Alexander, Ellen. Llama and the Great Flood: A Folktale
from Peru. New York: Thomas Y. Crowell, 1989. 39 p.
ISBN: 0-690-04729-0. $13.89. Gr. 2-4.

This is a simple retelling of the Peruvian myth about the
Great Flood, in which a llama warns his master of the coming destruction and leads him and his family to safety on
a high peak in the Andes. There is nothing particularly
exciting about the pastel watercolor illustrations except that
they do show life in the Andean mountains. Youngsters
studying Peru might enjoy reading or listening to this myth,
which was inspired by a collection of myths from Huarochirí,
a mountainous region northeast of Lima.

*Bateman, Penny. Aztecs and Incas: AD 1300-1531. Illus-
trated by Rob Shone. New York: Franklin Watts, 1988.
32 p. ISBN: 0-531-10622-5. $11.90. Gr. 4-7.

(See review under MEXICO.)

Bowne, Elizabeth. Cochá. Illustrated by Cathy Morrison.
Lakewood, CO: Bookmakers Guild, Inc., 1990. 106 p.
Hardcover. ISBN: 0-917665-40-6. $14.95. pap. ISBN:
0-917665-41-4. $9.95. Gr. 6-8.

Cochá, an Uru Indian boy, lives on floating islands on Lake
Titicaca, high in the Andes mountains of Peru. His father
is very sick, so Cochá has to go to the other side of the
island to try to sell fish to support the family. In the village, he is confronted by a threatening new way of life

which he doesn't understand. Readers interested in learning about the traditions and beliefs of the Urus might
find this story somewhat appealing. However, the contrived
characters and plot, as well as the author's constant
moralizing, do not result in an engaging novel.

Lye, Keith. Take a Trip to Peru. New York: Franklin
   Watts, 1987. 32 p. ISBN: 0-531-10363-3. $9.90. Gr.
   2-4.

Color photographs on every page and an easy-to-read text
introduce Peru, the third largest country in South America,
to young readers. It briefly discusses Peru's topography,
history, government, people, cities, agriculture, industries
and leisure activities. It is unfortunate that the photographs show only poor people--either from the cities or
the country of Peru.

Marrin, Albert. Inca and Spaniard: Pizarro and the Conquest
   of Peru. New York: Atheneum, 1989. 211 p. ISBN:
   0-689-31481-7. $13.95. Gr. 8-12.

The origins and culture of the Incas are presented in the
first part of this book, followed by basic facts about
Pizarro's life and the Spanish Conquest. Unfortunately,
the author dwells on negative or misunderstood aspects of
the Incas and Spaniards, presenting an unflattering view
of both cultures. For example, he elaborates on the Inca
practice of human sacrifice: "The victims were men, women,
and, above all children.... Many sacrificial victims were
chosen from among the Virgins of the Sun. All had to be
perfect; the smallest scratch or pimple made them un-
worthy.... On the day of sacrifice, the victims were fed
a hearty meal; mothers suckled their infants, so they
shouldn't go to the gods hungry or crying..." (p. 34).
The author has very few positive things to say about
Spaniards: "The younger Pizarros couldn't govern themselves, let alone a large city. To their greed for gold was
added a viciousness that would have brought swift punishment in Spain" (p. 131). Of course, these things are
true. But, instead of presenting the history of the Incas
and Spaniards with insight and understanding, this narrative degrades both cultures by omission and overemphasis.

Morrison, Marion. <u>An Inca Farmer</u>. Illustrated by Mark Bergin. (How They Lived) Vero Beach, FL: Rourke Enterprises, Inc., 1988. 32 p. ISBN: 0-86592-144-X. $12.66. Gr. 3-6.

Like other titles in this series, the visuals, which are richly textured illustrations complemented by excellent small photographs in color, are appealing and informative. They describe the life of a farmer in the Inca Empire before the arrival of the Spaniards. Simply and succinctly, the text tells about the daily life, food and drink, crime and punishment, festivals and gods, and other aspects of life during Inca times.

Odijk, Pamela. <u>The Incas</u>. (The Ancient World) Englewood Cliffs, NJ: Silver Burdett Press, 1990. 47 p. ISBN: 0-382-09889-7. $14.89. Gr. 4-7.

Like <u>The Aztecs</u>, another title in this series by the same author, this book fails to convey the greatness of Inca civilization. Through numerous facts, it monotonously describes Inca life, religion, history, arts and wars. Also, like many books about pre-Columbian people, it repeatedly reports on human sacrifices: "Most of the children who were sacrificed were buried alive, although some were killed in other ways" (p. 22). This is a sad introduction to the Incas, despite the excellent photographs in color and attractive presentation.

PUERTO RICO

Cofer, Judith Ortiz. The Line of the Sun. Athens: The
University of Georgia Press, 1989. 291 p. ISBN: 0-
8203-1106-5. $19.95. Gr. 9-adult.

The contrast of life between rural Puerto Rico and New
York City is dramatized in this fast-paced novel through
the adventures and tragedies of Guzmán, a young man who
was born in Puerto Rico, lived in New York City and was
misunderstood everywhere. Mature readers with a deep
attachment to Puerto Rico will be moved by the passions of
a pathetic human being and his caring family.

Cofer, Judith Ortiz. Silent Dancing: A Partial Remembrance
of a Puerto Rican Childhood. Houston, TX: Arte Público
Press, 1990. 158 p. ISBN: 1-55885-015-5. pap. $8.50.
Gr. 9-adult.

The trials and anxieties of a young girl growing up in two
cultures, Puerto Rico and New Jersey, are recounted in a
collection of sensitive short stories and poems that will
ring true to many readers. Female readers will be especially touched by the author's descriptions of her grandmother,
mother and other women who strongly influenced her
thoughts and attitudes toward women in Puerto Rican so-
ciety--both on the island and the mainland. Also of interest are the author's recollections of the English-speaking
and Spanish-speaking worlds and cultures with their con-
trasting values and attitudes. This is an honest autobiography depicting a young Puerto Rican girl confronting
her own family and culture.

*Delacre, Lulu. Las Navidades. Popular Christmas Songs from Latin America. New York: Scholastic, Inc., 1990. 33 p. ISBN: 0-590-43548-5. $12.95. Gr. PK-3.

Bilingual (English-Spanish) collection of popular Christmas songs, mainly from Puerto Rico, that beautifully conveys the joyous Christmas season as celebrated in Latin America. The warm, pastel illustrations depict well-known Puerto Rican, Mexican, and Venezuelan traditions. The music to each song appears at the end of the book. Puerto Rican families will certainly remember and rejoice.

*Delano, Jack. Puerto Rico Mio: Four Decades of Change/ Cuatro décadas de cambio. Photographs by Jack Delano. Washington, DC: Smithsonian Institution Press, 1990. 228 p. ISBN: 0-87474-389-3. pap. $24.95. Gr. 8-adult.

Puerto Rico in the 1940s is contrasted with Puerto Rico in the 1980s by photographer Jack Delano, who participated in the Farm Security Administration's documentary photo project begun in the 1930s. Outstanding black-and-white photographs depict the people, lifestyle, countryside and other views of Puerto Rico from a forty-year perspective. In contrast to the optimistic and spirited quality of the photographs, some readers may disagree with the negative tone of the four bilingual essays, which emphasize the detrimental effects of "North American imperialism" on the people of Puerto Rico. The most disturbing aspect of this book is the awkward Spanish translation and numerous Spanish grammatical and typographical mistakes, which could have been easily prevented.

Larsen, Ronald J. The Puerto Ricans in America. Minneapolis: Lerner Publications Company, 1989. 76 p. Hardcover ISBN: 0-8225-0238-0. $8.95; pap. ISBN: 0-8225-1036-7. $3.95. Gr. 6-9.

(See review under UNITED STATES.)

López, Alfredo. Doña Licha's Island: Modern Colonialism in Puerto Rico. Boston: South End Press, 1987. 178 p. ISBN: 0-89608-257-1. $9.00. Gr. 9-adult.

The author, who describes himself as a working journalist
for nearly twenty years, argues in a strong, passionate
manner that "[N]ever has the moment been so opportune
for the Puerto Rican independence movement--the only movement which advocates a clear alternative to what is becoming
an unbearable situation" (p. 156). After citing numerous
economic statistics and historical records, he concludes that
the only way Puerto Rico can avoid dependence is "by concentrating on its own survival, by vigorously pursuing a
balanced and independent economy, and by vigorously defending a democratic political structure" (p. 168). The
author's main contention is that "Puerto Rico has lived a
history in which its own social conditions and development
have constantly intertwined with, and been perverted by,
colonialism--first as a Spanish colony, then as a colony of
the United States" (p. 6). Supporters of the Puerto Rican
independence movement will agree with most of the author's
analyses; others will question; and others will condemn and
most certainly disapprove.

*Rohmer, Harriet, and Jesús Guerrero Rea, adapters. Atariba
and Niguayona: A Story from the Taino People of Puerto
Rico. Illustrated by Consuelo Mendez. Spanish version
by Rosalma Zubizarreta. ISBN: 0-89239-026-3.
*Rohmer, Harriet, and Mary Anchondo. How We Came to the
Fifth World/Cómo vinimos al quinto mundo: A Creation
Story from Ancient Mexico. Illustrated by Graciela Carrillo.
Spanish version by Harriet Rohmer and Rosalma Zubizarreta.
ISBN: 0-89239-024-7.
Ea. vol.: 24 p. (Tales of the Americas) San Francisco:
Children's Book Press, 1988. $10.95. Gr. 3-6.

There is definitely an improvement in the Spanish revisions
of these bilingual texts as compared to the previous editions.
The easy-flowing syntax of Spanish/English tales will now
appeal to readers of either language. The bright, bold,
colorful illustrations add a special Latin American zest to
lovers of primitive-style illustrations. Atariba and Niguayona
is a Taino legend from the people of Puerto Rico which tells
of a young boy's search for the tall caimoni tree whose
fruit will save Atariba's life. How We Came to the Fifth
World is an Aztec myth which recounts the creation and
destruction of the world by the deities of the four great
elements.

Walker, Paul Robert. Pride of Puerto Rico: The Life of
  Roberto Clemente. San Diego, CA: Harcourt Brace Jo-
  vanovich, 1988. 136 p. ISBN: 0-15-200562-5. $11.95.
  Gr. 4-7.

Baseball lovers will enjoy this simply written biography of
the great rightfielder of the Pittsburgh Pirates, Roberto
Clemente. Even though in the first part of the book the
author puts too much emphasis on the discrimination against
blacks and Hispanics prevalent in the U.S. during Clemente's
early years ("In the United States, blacks and whites
could not play on the same team, but in Puerto Rico a
player was judged by his talent, not his color" [p. 11]),
readers are nevertheless exposed to the trials and successes
of the renowned baseball player in an interesting manner.
At the end, the author again stresses Clemente's awards
together with his ethnic identity. He states: "... he
never thought these awards were just for himself. They
were for all the other Latin and black players who had
struggled to be accepted in the major leagues" (p. 123).
Young readers will appreciate Clemente's abilities as a baseball player and as a human being as depicted in this adula-
tory biography.

SPAIN

*Alvarado, Manuel. <u>Spain</u>. Photographs by David Cumming.
Illustrated by Malcolm S. Walker. New York: The Book-
wright Press, 1990. 48 p. ISBN: 0-531-18332-7. $12.40.
Gr. 5-8.

The geography, history, government, economy, culture
and people of Spain are introduced to young readers through
numerous color photographs and maps on every page, along
with a readable text. The author has done an excellent
job of portraying the many changes that have occurred in
Spain since the 1950s while preserving its many traditions
and beliefs.

*Anderson, David. <u>The Spanish Armada</u>. New York: Hamp-
stead Press, 1988. 48 p. ISBN: 0-531-19505-8. $11.90.
Gr. 5-8.

In a direct, easy-to-read manner, Anderson describes the
religious and territorial conflicts between England and
Spain as well as the events of 1588 and the Armada's
pathetic return to Spain. Numerous color drawings, charts,
and maps contribute immensely to readers' understanding
of this dramatic event in European history. It is important
to note that the author maintains an objective view regarding both sides and argues strongly that "... the Armada
campaign was just one event in a long war between England
and Spain. It settled nothing. In the long term the defeat of the Armada did not weaken Spain" (p. 44). And
concludes that: "The myths about the Armada began with
the propaganda that was published by the English government in 1588" (p. 44).

Codye, Corinn. Luis W. Alvarez. Illustrated by Bob Masheris.
   ISBN: 0-8172-3376-8.
_____. Queen Isabella I. Illustrated by Rick Whipple.
   ISBN: 0-8172-3380-6.
_____. Vilma Martinez. Illustrated by Susi Kilgore. ISBN:
   0-8172-3382-2.
De Varona, Frank. Bernardo de Gálvez. Illustrated by Tom
   Redman. ISBN: 0-8172-3379-2.
Gleiter, Jan. Benito Juárez. Illustrated by Francis Balistreri.
   ISBN: 0-8172-3381-4.
Sumption, Christine, and Kathleen Thompson. Carlos Finlay.
   Illustrated by Les Didier. ISBN: 0-8172-3378-4.
Thompson, Kathleen. Pedro Menéndez de Avilés. Illustrated
   by Charles Shaw. ISBN: 0-8172-3383-0.
_____. Sor Juana Inés de la Cruz. Illustrated by Rick
   Karpinski. ISBN: 0-8172-3377-6.
   Ea. vol.: 32 p. (Raintree Hispanic Stories) Milwaukee:
   Raintree Publishers, 1990. $15.33. Gr. 3-5.

Through the lives of eight Hispanic men and women from
the United States, Cuba, Spain and Mexico, young readers
will learn that through dedication and hard work these
people were able "to change the world to make it a better
place." An easy-to-read bilingual (English/Spanish) text
on every page and soft pastel watercolor illustrations high-
light the important achievements of these scientists, ruler,
lawyer, governor, president, poet, and explorer. Despite
their didactic intent, these simple biographies may be just
right for young readers in search of role models.

Connatty, Mary. The Armada. Illustrated by Richard Hook
   and others. New York: Warwick Press, 1987. 40 p.
   ISBN: 0-531-19030-7. $13.90. Gr. 5-8.

In a chatty, almost too casual manner, Connatty describes
the events that led to the dispatch of the Spanish Armada,
the actual engagements and the Armada's difficult return
to Spain. The striking, colorful illustrations of the people,
places and ships of the time as well as the clear charts
and maps will undoubtedly appeal to young readers. What
this narrative does not do, however, is provide a thought-
ful discussion of the issues that resulted as a consequence
of this extraordinary event in European history.

*A Day in the Life of Spain. Edited by Rick Smolan and
  David Cohen. New York: Collins Publishers, 1988. 220 p.
  ISBN: 0-00-217967-9. $45. Gr. 7-adult.

On May 7, 1987, "one hundred of the world's leading photo-
journalists" were positioned throughout Spain to capture a
typical Spanish day on film. The intent of the editors was
to show an "honest look at Spain in the 1980s, not just
another book of pretty picture postcards." The results
are a stunning view of Spain through exquisite color photographs of the people and the countryside. With very few
exceptions, the photographs and brief narratives do an
excellent job of depicting the life and mood of modern Spain,
including its contrasts and traditions.

Delibes, Miguel. The Stuff of Heroes. Translated from the
  Spanish by Frances M. López-Morillas. New York: Pan-
  theon Books, 1990. 293 p. ISBN: 0-394-57746-9. $22.95.
  Gr. 9-adult.

Enthusiasts of the Spanish Civil War will be pleased by this
coming-of-age novel in which Gervasio, the youngest son
of an old Spanish aristocratic family, deals with his own
conflicting thoughts and feelings regarding heroism, bravery
and loyalty. Family quarrels, political opinions and the
peculiarities of life in Spain in the 1930s are explored with
tact and understanding, especially as they affect an adolescent boy who learns that "there are times in life when the
line between heroism and treachery is as thin as a sheet
of cigarette paper" (p. 72). Most readers, however, will
find this novel slow reading and restricted in its appeal.

Finkelstein, Norman H. The Other 1492: Jewish Settlement
  in the New World. New York: Charles Scribner's Sons,
  1989. 100 p. ISBN: 0-684-18913-5. $12.95. Gr. 5-8.

In a simple narrative, the author discusses the contributions
of Sephardic Jews to Spanish culture and society; their
persecution, conversion and exile from Spain; and their
settlement in the New World. Engaging black-and-white
reproductions of art works and manuscripts of the period
add interest to the text. This is an interesting discussion
of the Spanish monarchs Ferdinand and Isabella, the

Inquisition and the Catholic Church from a Jewish perspective. The following could be the author's summary:
"Yet the presence and success of the proud Jewish popu-
latin in America must be credited to the bravery, devotion,
or perhaps luck of the original Jewish settlers of Spanish
and Portuguese heritage" (p. 90).

*Fusi, J. P. Franco: A Biography. Translated by Felipe
Fernández-Armesto. New York: Harper & Row Publishers,
Inc., 1988. 202 p. ISBN: 0-06-433127-X. $25.00. Gr.
9-adult.

The author states in the introduction that this "biographical essay [is] intended as a short critical survey of Franco's
life." So, in a balanced and concise manner, Fusi reas-
sesses the complex and elusive figure who ruled Spain for
almost forty years until his death in 1975. Readers interested in understanding the complexities of modern Spain
and Franco's controversial regime will find this book intriguing and thought provoking. Critics and admirers of
Franco will be both pleased and provoked by Fusi's analysis. For example, he states that in the period after 1964-
65 "... Franco began to take on the image of a weak and
frail old man. In combination with his courtesy and affa-
bility, this gave him an air of mellowness, even kindness,
ill suited to the reality of the despotic, oppressive power,
which he continued to wield until 1975" (p. 128).

*Garza, Hedda. Francisco Franco. (World Leaders Past &
Present) New York: Chelsea House Publishers, 1987.
112 p. ISBN: 0-87754-524-3. $16.95. Gr. 6-12.

This is a well-written description of the life and times of
Francisco Franco, who ruled Spain for "almost 40 years,
crushing it under an iron jackboot of censorship, torture,
and death" (p. 19). Young adults will definitely get a
feeling of the horrors of the Spanish Civil War as well as
the international politics that surrounded Franco's early
successes. Numerous black-and-white photographs on almost
every page and a vivid narrative provide readers with a
formidable indictment and "a sorrowful reminder of a bloody
civil war and of the tyrant who ruled Spain for 36 years"
(p. 107). Franco's admirers will obviously disagree, but

most readers will concur and appreciate this revealing picture of Spanish fascism and one of its best known leaders.

Gleiter, Jan, and Kathleen Thompson. David Farragut. Illustrated by Francis Balistreri. ISBN: 0-8172-2904-3.
_____. Diego Rivera. Illustrated by Yoshi Miyake. ISBN: 0-8172-2908-6.
_____. Junípero Serra. Illustrated by Charles Shaw. ISBN: 0-8172-2909-4.
Ea. vol.: 32 p. Milwaukee: Raintree Publishers, 1989. $15.99. Gr. 3-5.

The lives of three notable Hispanics from Mexico, the United States, and Spain are briefly narrated in these bilingual (Spanish/English) books. Even though there is nothing particularly exciting about these titles, they do provide basic facts about the lives and accomplishments of these three Hispanic men who excelled in the U.S. Civil War, in the arts and in the development of missions in California. Unfortunately, these books will remind many readers of their social studies textbooks, especially the bland watercolor illustrations and the lackluster Spanish and English texts. The content, however, is inspiring and true.

*Goodwin, Godfrey. Islamic Spain. (Architectural Guide for Travelers) San Francisco: Chronicle Books, 1990. 150 p. ISBN: 0-87701-692-5. pap. $14.95. Gr. 9-adult.

The author, a professor of art and architectural history, reveals his enthusiasm regarding Islamic contributions to Spain and its culture in this concise guide with numerous excellent black-and-white photographs. It is written for travelers and organized by such centers as Sevilla, Córdoba, and Granada; where no one city can serve as a focus, sites are listed under province. Non-travelers also will be able to appreciate the beauty of the Islamic presence in Spain and to understand the cross-fertilization which "was so important to the marriage of Western and Eastern ideas" (p. vii).

Huffington, Arianna Stassinopoulos. Picasso: Creator and

Destroyer. New York: Simon and Schuster, 1988. 558 p.
ISBN: 0-671-45446-3. $33.95. Gr. 10-adult.

All of Picasso's negative qualities are detailed in this compelling biography of the well-known artist. Readers interested in a discussion of Picasso's creative output will
need to look elsewhere. This is basically a fast-moving
account of Picasso's numerous romantic/sexual liaisons and
marriages in which "the monumental egoist" and "sadistic
manipulator" was really "a man unable to love, intent on
seduction not in the search for love, not even in the desire
to possess, but in a compulsion to destroy" (p. 10). Of
course, the author provides strong evidence incriminating
Picasso, the destroyer, such as the suicides of his second
wife, his grandson, and one of his mistresses, as well as
the "psychic disintegration" of his first wife and the
nervous breakdown of Dora Maar, another mistress. Some
readers will be engrossed by this account of Picasso's
tragic personal relationships; others will be disturbed by
the author's psychosexual indictments and accusations which
show little sympathy or understanding.

*James, Ian. Inside Spain. New York: Franklin Watts, 1989.
32 p. ISBN: 0-531-10834-1. $11.40. Gr. 4-8.

Numerous excellent photographs in color and a simple, direct text make this an excellent introduction to the land,
history, people, arts, economy, industry and other aspects of Spain. Readers looking for a contemporary view
of Spain will find this attractive book difficult to surpass,
despite such statements as the following: "In 1985, bullfighting attracted 36.1 million spectators, though an in-
creasing number of Spaniards are opposed to bullfighting"
(p. 19).

*Katz, William Loren, and Marc Crawford. The Lincoln Brigade:
A Picture History. New York: Atheneum, 1989. 84 p.
ISBN: 0-689-31408-X. $14.95. Gr. 7-10.

This book is aptly dedicated to the Americans who fought
to save democracy in Spain and to warn of the Nazi danger.
Numerous black-and-white photographs and a readable text
describe the individuals who chose to volunteer, Spain in

the 1930s, the Great Depression in the United States, life
behind the lines, the retreat, and the survivors' triumphal
return to Spain in October 1986. This is a lively picture
history of the American volunteers who went to Spain to
become the Abraham Lincoln Brigade.

Kemp, Peter. The Campaign of the Spanish Armada New
York: Facts on File Publications, 1988. 160 p. ISBN:
0-8160-1828-6. $24.95. Gr. 9-adult.

The campaign of the Spanish Armada is narrated in a
flowing text and exquisitely illustrated with black-and-
white and color reproductions of contemporary paintings,
artifacts and charts. The author provides enough background information to excite young readers about this
great military and naval campaign that proved to be an
important turning point in the history of Spain and England.
In contrast to many contemporary English-speaking authors
who try to maintain an objective perspective regarding
sixteenth-century Spain, Kemp does not seem to be bothered by his obvious bias. For example, the following is
his description of the Duke of Medina Sidonia, the Spanish
Commander-in-Chief, "On the basis of his letters to the
King it is impossible to think of him but as a man of mean
spirit" (p. 70). And, "A Spanish victory would mean a
Europe under Spanish dominion, half a continent held in
thrall to the inquisitorial doctrine of Roman Catholicism
and the torture and burning of heretics" (p. 127). It
is important to note, too, that the name of Philip II's
Palace of the Escurial [sic] (pp. 53, 69, 136) is misspelled
throughout the book.

Landis, Arthur H. Death in the Olive Groves: American
Volunteers in the Spanish Civil War, 1936-1939. New
York: Paragon House Publishers, 1988. 254 p. ISBN:
1-55778-051-X. $18.95. Gr. 9-adult.

The formation of the Abraham Lincoln Brigade, which
fought to support the Spanish Republic against the Fascist
Falenge in the Spanish Civil War, is retold in this condensed version from an earlier book, The Abraham Lincoln
Brigade, by the same author. By quoting extensively
from contemporary newspapers and magazine articles, Landis

provides a testimony of the courage and suffering of the
3200 Americans who made up this brigade. He states:
"A final summation of the achievements of the men of the
Abraham Lincoln Brigade both in Spain and in World War
II would suggest that in battles fought, in men lost, and
in honors received, they might easily surpass any other
group of fighting men in the military history of the United
States" (p. 223). Serious students of the Spanish Civil
War might enjoy these reminiscences.

*Lye, Keith. Passport to Spain. New York: Franklin Watts,
Inc., 1987. 48 p. ISBN: 0-531-10402-8. $11.40. Gr.
4-7.

Numerous facts about the people and the country of Spain
are included in this British publication. It is especially
useful as a basic introduction to the land, cities, industry,
tourism, people and the arts of modern Spain because of
its abundance of colorful photographs, maps, charts as
well as its simple, direct text. Readers interested in an
up-to-date view of Spain will not be disappointed.

Macdonald, Fiona. Drake and the Armada. Illustrated by
Chris Molan. New York: Hampstead Press, 1988. 48 p.
ISBN: 0-531-19504-X. $11.90. Gr. 5-8.

The life story of Sir Francis Drake, the famous sixteenth-
century sailor, explorer, battle commander, and English
hero who helped defeat the Spanish Armada in 1588, is
depicted in a lively narrative with exciting watercolor illustrations. The brevity of each chapter and the lack of
extraneous information make this biography a good selection for introducing young readers to the life and times
of Sir Francis Drake.

*MacDonald, Patricia A. Pablo Picasso. Englewood Cliffs,
NJ: Silver Burdett Press, 1990. 128 p. ISBN: 0-382-
09903-6. $17.98. Gr. 7-12.

The life, time and works of the renowned artist Pablo
Picasso are examined in a concise, interesting narrative.
The author must be commended for stressing only important

aspects of and influences on Picasso's life, thereby allow-
ing readers to understand Picasso's creative genius.
Numerous black-and-white and eight full color reproductions with simple, excellent descriptions of each work add
to the readers' comprehension of Picasso's legacy.

*Marvin, Garry. Bullfight. New York: Basil Blackwell,
Inc., 1988. 226 p. ISBN: 0-631-15471-X. $18.95. Gr.
9-adult.

Anyone interested in understanding the meaning and nature
of the "corrida," especially in the English-speaking world,
should read this insightful account of the bullfight. The
author, an anthropologist, does not pretend to write an
ethnographic study of the "corrida," but rather his narrative "concentrates on the meaning and nature of the
'corrida,' particularly in terms of its structure; ... an
analysis of the setting of the event, the role of the human
performers and the nature of their performance, the role
of the animals, the relation between those animals and the
humans, and its character as a celebration ..." (p. viii).
This is indeed a most complete description of the world
of bullfighting written by a man who neither condemns
nor acclaims but truly understands the excitement of
"corridas."

*Miller, Arthur. Spain. (Places and Peoples of the World)
New York: Chelsea House, 1989. 120 p. ISBN: 1-
55546-795-4. $12.95. Gr. 4-7.

The history, topography, people, culture, economy, industry, and politics of Spain are described in a most comprehensive and well-written narrative. In contrast to many
books that provide a superficial view of Spain, this one
explains many characteristics of the people and country
with great understanding. The following is an example
which young readers can relate to: "Many people think
of Spain as a land of bullfights, castles, and 'senoritas'
[sic] swirling in a flamenco dance. These remnants of
old Spain still exist, but today a Spaniard is more likely
to attend a soccer match than a bullfight, to vacation in
a high-rise apartment instead of in a castle, and to dance
at a disco instead of to the twang of a guitar" (p. 16).

Black-and-white and color photos add interest to the narrative.

*Miró, Joan. Joan Miró: A Retrospective. New Haven, CT: Yale University Press/Solomon R. Guggenheim Museum, 1987. 268 p. ISBN: 0-300-04073-3. $50.00. Gr. 10-adult.

Joan Miró's spontaneity and love of life are evident in this major retrospective which reproduces 150 of his paintings, objects, collages, ceramics and works on paper. The excellent quality of the reproductions; four informative, scholarly essays on the art of Joan Miró; and a personal memoir by the artist provide the reader/viewer with a joyous view of the life and work of the twentieth-century master from Catalonia, Spain. Artists-to-be should be inspired by the achievements of this exuberant artist as depicted in these pages.

*Padfield, Peter. Armada: A Celebration of the Four Hundredth Anniversary of the Defeat of the Spanish Armada, 1588-1988. Annapolis, MD: Naval Institute Press, 1988. 208 p. ISBN: 0-87021-006-8. $24.95. Gr. 9-adult.

The Spanish and English campaigns of 1587-88, their preparation, course and conclusion are narrated by a well-known naval historian and biographer in a meticulous text. The exciting narrative is greatly enhanced by gorgeous color and black-and-white illustrations of the people, places, battleships as well as excellent reproductions of sixteenth-century maps and charts. This is both a fascinating account of the defeat of the Spanish Armada and a beautiful large-format book that brings to life one of the greatest defeats of all times.

*Pellicer, Maria Eugenia D. Spanish Food and Drink. (Food and Drink) New York: The Bookwright Press, 1988. 48 p. ISBN: 0-531-18173-1. $11.90. Gr. 5-8.

Young people are introduced to Spain and its people through its food and its ways of eating. Attractive photographs in color further explain Spain's agriculture, food industry, stores, regional specialties, fishing, festive foods and eating habits. In addition, it includes a few recipes for Spanish dishes such as "paella" and "churros." This is a delightful way to introduce students to Spain.

*Raboff, Ernest. Diego Rodriguez de Silva y Velásquez. ISBN: 0-06-446073-8.
*_____. Pablo Picasso. ISBN: 0-06-446067-3. Ea. vol.: [28 p.] (Art for Children) New York: Harper & Row Publishers, 1987 & 1988. $5.95. Gr. 3-6.

Excellent brief biographies of Velásquez and Picasso that tell about key aspects of their life and work. Numerous color reproductions and simply written critical interpretations give young readers a basic understanding of these artists' creative achievements. The only disagreeable aspect of these paperback publications is that the handwritten text, printed in various colors, is not pleasant to read.

*Say, Allen. El Chino. Boston: Houghton Mifflin Company, 1990. 32 p. ISBN: 0-395-52023-1. $14.95. Gr. 3-5.

This is a touching biography about Bill Wong, a Chinese American who became a famous bullfighter in Spain. Young readers will be inspired by Billy's determination to become a matador. He was often told: "Only the Spaniards can become true matadors." Yet, he persevered and finally succeeded. The lively watercolor illustrations perfectly complement the easy-to-read narrative.

*Venezia, Mike. Picasso. (Getting to Know the World's Greatest Artists) Illustrated by the author. Chicago: Childrens Press, 1988. 32 p. ISBN: 0-516-02271-7. $9.95. Gr. 3-6.

In a lighthearted manner, this simply written and profusely illustrated biography introduces young readers to the life and work of Pablo Picasso. Some readers might object to the author's use of cartoons to emphasize controversial aspects of Picasso's work, but the cleverly done cartoons do an excellent job of explaining longstanding debates regarding Picasso's work to children. In addition, the full-

color reproductions of the actual paintings discussed in
the narrative provide youngsters with an inspiring view of
Picasso's various periods or styles.

White, Florence Meiman. The Story of Junípero Serra, Brave
Adventurer. Illustrated by Stephen Marchesi. New York:
Dell Publishing Co., 1987. 86 p. ISBN: 0-440-42495-
X. $2.95. Gr. 4-6.

Father Junípero Serra, who founded the first nine California
missions in the years 1769 through 1782, is introduced to
young readers in this easy-to-read biography. Black-and-
white pencil illustrations further add to the readers' understanding of the life and times of this daring Spanish
missionary. Even though one should question the overly
positive description of Father Serra, this biography does
provide an exciting introduction to the live of Spanish
missionaries in the eighteenth century in California.

Woods, Geraldine. Spain: A Shining New Democracy. (Discovering Our Heritage) Minneapolis: Dillon Press, Inc.,
1987. 166 p. ISBN: 0-87518-340-5. $12.95. Gr. 5-8.

Spain is introduced to young people through its arts, history, holidays, homelife, and educational system. Up-to-
date information and outstanding color photographs make
this book particularly useful for this age group. It is unfortunate, however, that the author resorted to an overly
cute writing style often patronizing the readers. The last
chapter, "Adventure in America," discusses the contributions that Spaniards have made in the United States. But
here, too, the author's writing style is either too cute or
oversimplified: "Unfortunately, besides sharing television
shows and newspapers, Hispanic-Americans also share
something else with Spanish-Americans--prejudice" (p. 147).

UNITED STATES

Aaseng, Nathan. <u>Jose Canseco: Baseball's 40-40 Man</u>. Minneapolis: Lerner Publications Company, 1989. 56 p.
ISBN: 0-8225-0493-6. $8.95. Gr. 3-6.

Fans of the star outfielder of the Oakland Athletics, Jose
Canseco, will find many facts about their hero's baseball
career in this focused sports biography. The only references to Canseco's personal life are one baseball writer's
recent claim that "Canseco's muscular body had been built
by using drugs called steroids" (p. 7), and a brief discussion on its controversy; one paragraph about his Hispanic name and place of birth (Havana, Cuba); and one
reference to his marriage "to Esther Haddad on October 25"
(p. 52). Otherwise, this is pure baseball talk with a chart
about Canseco's career statistics as well as numerous black-
and-white photos of Canseco playing baseball.

Alarcón, Francisco X. <u>Body in Flames/Cuerpo en Llamas</u>.
Translated by Francisco Aragon. San Francisco: Chronicle Books, 1990. 107 p. ISBN: 0-87701-718-2. pap.
$8.95. Gr. 9-adult.

The Latino experience in the United States is recounted in
these moving bilingual poems written by a contemporary
Latino poet, native of Los Angeles. Interestingly, the
poet does not use periods or commas. His most touching
poems tell about his grandmother in a neighborhood in
Los Angeles, a mother's advice, and his sister's small but
fateful victory. Unfortunately, the Spanish translation
does not do justice to the original poems. The Spanish
version include numerous grammatical and spelling mistakes.

*Anderson, Joan. Spanish Pioneers of the Southwest. Photographs by George Acona. New York: E. P. Dutton, 1989. [30 p.] ISBN: 0-525-67264-8. $14.95. Gr. 3-6.

The life of a pioneer family in a Spanish settlement in New Mexico during the eighteenth century is recreated through sensitive black-and-white photographs and a spirited narrative. This is indeed a most informative photo essay that truly depicts the hard work, harsh living conditions and strong Hispanic traditions of those early settlers. There is only one disturbing aspect in this otherwise excellent book. The narrative includes too many Spanish words intermingled in the narrative. Of course, this accentuates the Hispanic flavor of the book, but it is also a condescending way to treat the Spanish language.

Ashabranner, Brent. The Vanishing Border: A Photographic Journey Along Our Frontier with Mexico. Photographs by Paul Conklin. New York: Dodd, Mead & Company, 1987. 175 p. ISBN: 0-396-08900-3. $14.95. Gr. 7-12.

In a lively and optimistic manner, the author discusses life on the U.S. side of the two-thousand mile border between Mexico and the U.S. The author uses a few simple statistics and numerous personal observations to explain the reasons why illegal aliens, mostly Mexicans, are coming to the United States in unprecedented numbers. He also discusses the need for cheap labor by U.S. industries and agriculture as well as the interrelationship between the two countries. The best part of this book is the insights the author provides about life in the various regions along the U.S. southern border. These are further supported by exquisite black-and-white photographs of the people and the countryside. Readers must realize, however, that this book provides only a superficial view of the serious problems between Mexico and the U.S. and a most cursory and simplistic review of the issues and potential problems as a result of the October 17, 1986, Immigration Law. In addition, most of the Spanish words used in the book are misspelled, e.g., "Morrelos" [sic] (p. 111) and "chilie rellenos" [sic] (p. 129).

Beardsley, John, and Jane Livingston. Hispanic Art in the

United States: Thirty Contemporary Painters & Sculptors.
New York: Abbeville Press, 1987. 260 p. ISBN: 0-
89659-688-5. $45.00. Gr. 10-adult.

Three scholarly essays which introduce contemporary Hispanic art in the United States, numerous excellent color
photographs of the work of thirty artists, and brief biographies of these artists make this volume of special interest to serious art students. Only a few of the artists--
Manuel Neri and Robert Graham--are well known; most,
however, are little known both to the critics and to the
general public. The stylistic diversity and variety of selected contemporary Hispanic artists are well represented
in this attractive publication.

Bode, Janet. Different Worlds: Interracial and Cross-
    Cultural Dating. New York: Franklin Watts, 1989. 120 p.
    ISBN: 0-531-10663-2. $12.90. Gr. 7-12.

The complex issues involved in interracial and cross-
cultural dating among teenagers are discussed in this easy-
to-read narrative. It includes a simple but clear explana-
tion of prejudice as well as discussions on parental reactions,
peer pressure and psychological motivations. Of special
interest to adolescents may be the numerous stories of
couples from Mexican American, Puerto Rican, Chicano,
Hispanic, black, Chinese or other backgrounds and how
they deal with these issues.

Caroli, Betty Boyd. Immigrants Who Returned Home. (The
    Peoples of North America) New York: Chelsea House
    Publishers, 1990. 188 p. ISBN: 0-87754-864-1. $17.95.
    Gr. 7-10.

In a highly readable text and numerous black-and-white
and color photographs and cartoons, this book considers
how the members of some of America's most prominent immigrant groups decide the question of whether their stay in
the United States is permanent or whether they return to
their homelands. As a general introduction to this topic,
this book is indeed worthwhile and informative. Unfortunately, readers interested in learning about Hispanics
who return home will be disappointed. In chapter one,

it includes the following generalization: "Today, hundreds of thousands of Central Americans, fleeing poverty and political oppression, risk their lives to reach the United States, only to be denied legal entry; should they enter illegally, they are often relegated to a life of poverty and exploitation" (p. 15). And, the important issue of Mexican migration is briefly covered on three pages of the last chapter.

Catalano, Julie. The Mexican Americans. (The Peoples of North America) New York: Chelsea House Publishers, 1988. 95 p. ISBN: 0-87754-857-9. $16.95. Gr. 4-8.

The experiences and contributions of the Mexican Americans in the United States are described in a straightforward narrative with numerous black-and-white and a few color photographs. The text emphasizes the abuses and discrimination that people of Mexican descent have suffered throughout their history. There is no question that the main purpose of this book is to develop a sense of pride in Mexican Americans; yet, the strictly didactic approach of this book and the numerous spelling mistakes--"Fiesta Navidena" [sic] (p. 70), "city of Pueblo" [sic] (p. 71), "musica nortena" [sic] (p. 73)--are not enlightening.

Cervantes, Esther De Michael, and Alex Cervantes. Barrio Ghosts. Syracuse, NY: New Readers Press, 1988. 79 p. ISBN: 0-88336-315-1. pap. $3.75. Gr. 6-9.

Collection of five ghost stories with a strong Hispanic flavor and lots of action. They deal with high-interest topics for teenagers, such as a phantom low rider, a rock 'n' roll ghost, "La Llorona" (the beautiful ghost woman who weeps for the loss of her children), a teenager that becomes a cat, and a ghost dancer. This is easy reading for those interested in brief stories.

Chavez, Angelico. The Short Stories of Fray Angelico Chavez. Edited by Genaro M. Padilla. Albuquerque: University of New Mexico Press, 1987. 139 p. ISBN: 0-8263-0950-X. $9.95. Gr. 9-adult.

Fourteen stories set in New Mexico beginning in colonial
days up to the middle of the twentieth century are included in this publication. Some readers may enjoy the
allegorical style of these stories which tell of the tragic
events, hopes, spiritual temptations and moral dilemmas of
the Indo-Hispano people of New Mexico's villages and
towns. Of special interest to young adults is the story
"A Romeo and Juliet Story in Early New Mexico," which
has "the more pleasant features of Shakespeare's Romeo
and Juliet--and some of the heart tragedy, too, even if
there were no deaths or carnage to mar or prevent a happy ending" (p. 37).

Chavez, Tibo J. New Mexican Folklore of the Rio Abajo.
Illustrated by Reggie Chavez. Santa Fe, NM: William
Gannon, 1987. 69 p. ISBN: 0-88307-671-3. $7.95. Gr.
9-adult.

It is unfortunate that this book which was first published
in 1972 has been reprinted in 1987 with the same grammatical and spelling mistakes in the Spanish language.
The first part describes in a chatty and informal manner
the medicinal herbs used in the middle Rio Grande area
of New Mexico. The author states that "this is not intended to be a scientific expertise [sic] on the subject of
remedios" (p. 3) but rather he relates what was told to
him "by the curanderas and those residents of the Rio
Abajo that practiced the use of the healing herbs and age-
old healing practices and traditions" (p. 3). As such,
this section may be of some interest to those interested
in how common remedies were used in New Mexico. But,
there are so many negative aspects about this publication
that readers should look elsewhere for information on New
Mexican folklore. As stated earlier, the numerous spelling
and grammatical mistakes in Spanish in the section on
Spanish proverbs are unparalleled; the blurry black-and-
white photos of medicinal herbs and "curanderas" are
worthless; and the essay on the early practice of witch-
craft in New Mexico is trite and poorly written. Definitely
a low-quality publication.

Clark, Asa Bement. Travels in Mexico and California: Comprising a Journal of a Tour from Brazos Santiago, Through

Central Mexico, by Way of Monterrey, Chihuahua, the
Country of the Apaches, and the River Gila to the Mining
Districts of California. Edited by A. B. Clarke. College
Station: Texas A&M University Press, 1988. 143 p.
ISBN: 0-89096-354-1. $17.50. Gr. 8-adult.

(See review under MEXICO.)

Codye, Corinn. Luis W. Alvarez. Illustrated by Bob Mash-
eris. ISBN: 0-8172-3376-8.
_____. Vilma Martinez. Illustrated by Susi Kilgore.
ISBN: 0-8172-3382-2.
Ea. vol.: 32 p. (Raintree Hispanic Stories) Milwaukee:
Raintree Publishers, 1990. $15.33. Gr. 3-5.

(See review under SPAIN: Codye, Corinn....)

Coles, Robert. The Old Ones of New Mexico. Revised edition; Albuquerque: University of New Mexico Press, 1989.
74 p. ISBN: 0-8263-1137-7. pap. $19.95. Gr. 9-
adult.

Two new brief prefaces, one by the author and one by
the photographer, are the additions to this revised edition
which first appeared in 1973. Robert Coles states that
through this work he came to see that "there is a remarkable strength and vitality" in these elderly people, even
though "others from the Anglo world might consider them
aloof, old-fashioned, superstitious, all too set in their
ways" (p. xiii). So, through "several" visits, no standard
questions and his "passable" Spanish, he translated the
speech he heard "in such a way that its flavor and tone
come across to the middle-class 'Anglo' people who will
read this book" (p. xv). Perhaps some readers will be
interested in Coles' views of the five "old ones" and their
families who he met in New Mexico, or others will appreciate the forty black-and-white portraits of elderly Hispanics of New Mexico. Most readers, however, will be
disappointed if they are looking for a true depiction of
the thoughts and feelings of elderly Hispanics from New
Mexico.

Cook, Bruce. <u>Mexican Standoff</u>. New York: Franklin Watts, 1988. 235 p. ISBN: 0-531-15089-5. $16.95. Gr. 9-adult.

Lots of action, a kind Mexican American private detective, a pregnant Mexican prostitute, drug smuggling and violence combine to make this detective novel set in Culiacán, Mexico, and Los Angeles engrossing reading. Perhaps some adults might object exposing young adults to explicit sex talk or to the activities inside a house of prostitution, but these are certainly needed in the excitement of this spicy, fast-reading novel. Others might object to the depiction of the drug scene in Mexico, but no one expects that to be uplifting or elegant.

Didion, Joan. <u>Miami</u>. New York: Simon & Schuster, 1987. 238 p. ISBN: 0-671-64664-8. $17.45. Gr. 9-adult.

The influence of the Cuban Americans in the city of Miami is described in a direct and fast-paced narrative. Didion emphasizes the deep sense of betrayal felt by many Cuban exiles at the hands of the U.S. government beginning with President Kennedy up to President Reagan. Many readers will disagree with Didion's analysis of the Miami Cuban mind, but most readers will concur with her descriptions of Miami in 1986: "The entire tone of the city, the way people looked and talked and met one another, was Cuban. The very image the city had begun presenting of itself, what was then its newfound glamour, its 'hotness' (hot colors, hot vice, shady dealings under the palm trees) was that of prerevolutionary Havana, as perceived by Americans" (p. 52).

*Eisenhower, John S. D. <u>So Far from God: The U.S. War with Mexico, 1846-1848</u>. New York: Random House, Inc., 1989. 436 p. ISBN: 0-394-56051-5. $24.95. Gr. 9-adult.

The author, a distinguished military historian and the son of Dwight D. Eisenhower, has written a lively, engaging narrative about the U.S.-Mexico War taking into account many personal and political realities from both sides of the border. Eisenhower is quick to note the egotism and

overbearing arrogance in many of the U.S. politicians and
military leaders. He also cites the corruption, abuse and
incompetence of their Mexican counterparts. He acknowl-
edges that the United States has not been blameless in
its actions towards Mexico yet, he also states that "To the
student of today the fate of Mexico is sad, for the Mexicans were victims of both their history and Yankee expan-
sionism. But that sadness need not be exacerbated by
excessive shame for the conduct of the United States, because Mexico's disorganization, corruption, and weakness
created a power vacuum that would inevitably have been
filled by some predator--if not the United States, then
Britain, less likely France, and even, remotely, Russia"
(p. xx). Some readers may be turned off by the detailed
descriptions of numerous battle scenes. Nevertheless,
this balanced account of the U.S. war with Mexico is indeed
fascinating reading.

First Encounters: Spanish Explorations in the Caribbean and
the United States, 1492-1570. Ed. by Jerald T. Milanich
and Susan Milbrath. Gainesville, FL: University of
Florida Press, 1989. 222 p. Hardcover ISBN: 0-8130-
0946-4. $44.95; pap. ISBN: 0-8130-0947-2. $16.95.
Gr. 9-adult.

The story of Spain's attempts to explore and settle the
Caribbean and the United States is narrated in thirteen
chapters written by professors and researchers as an ac-
companiment to the Florida Museum of Natural History's
traveling exhibit of the same name. Serious students of
the Spanish explorations and its impact on native New World
peoples will be interested in these readable essays illustrated with outstanding black-and-white and color photographs of maps, artifacts and paintings. This study places
the exploits of Columbus, de Soto, and other early explorers in a historical and cultural context. It also explains the history of Spain at the time of Columbus and the
Indian responses to European contact.

Garcia, Guy. Skin Deep. New York: Farrar, Straus, Giroux, 1988. 186 p. ISBN: 0-374-26573-9. $16.95. Gr.
9-adult.

David Loya, a second generation Mexican American from an East Los Angeles barrio who earned a Harvard law degree, is a young successful lawyer at a prestigious law firm in New York City. Suddenly, he gets a call from an old Anglo friend from Los Angeles asking him to assist him in a case of Chicano blackmail. David is thus thrust into a dangerous situation in which an innocent Mexican girl was abused by an all-powerful California politician. David's trip back home forces him to rethink his own values and goals. Despite the action, violence and intrigue, some readers may be overwhelmed by the superfluous symbolism and uncalled-for pre-Columbian and folkloric passages interspersed in the novel.

*Garza, Carmen Lomas. Family Pictures/Cuadros de familia. Illustrated by the author. Spanish version: Rosalma Zubizarreta. San Francisco: Children's Book Press, 1990. 32 p. ISBN: 0-89239-050-6. $12.95. Gr. 3-6.

Vibrant, detailed illustrations and an easy-to-read bilingual (English/Spanish) narrative relate the author's experiences as a young Hispanic girl in Texas. Readers will savor fiestas, family gatherings, holidays, religion and other activities of a closely-knit Mexican American family through this beautifully designed picture book.

Gaskin, Carol, and George Guthridge. Death Mask of Pancho Villa. Illustrated by Kenneth Huey. (Time Machine 19) New York: Bantam Books, 1987. 126 p. ISBN: 0-553-26674-8. $2.50. Gr. 5-8.

The mission for readers of this participation story is "to find Pancho Villa's death mask--before his enemies can destroy it--and to hide it in a safe place." Readers in search of lots of action will certainly find it during the Mexican Revolution, and in this book. The black-and-white line illustrations are sloppy and crude; and the map of Mexico is inaccurate. One would hope that readers will select other books about the Mexican Revolution.

*Gernand, Renée. The Cuban Americans. (The Peoples of North America) New York: Chelsea House Publishers, 1988. 110 p. ISBN: 0-87754-869-2. $16.95. Gr. 5-10.

The success of the Cuban immigrants in the U.S. is described in this well-written introduction to Cuban Americans.
It includes chapters on the history, as well as the political
and economic upheavals that occurred in Cuba up to the
1960s, when a great number of Cuban exiles arrived in
the U.S. The most valuable aspect of this book, however,
is the author's objectivity in dealing with Cuban-American
achievements and their struggle for acceptance in the
United States. The following are two examples of the
author's descriptions of sensitive issues: "During the re-
cession of the mid-1970s, Miami was the only major U.S.
city with an increase in per capita income, a boom it owed
to its Cuban Americans. Few of Miami's longtime residents
reacted with gratitude to this economic turnabout and, in
fact, many grumbled at the Cubans' growing prosperity
and power in Dade County, where Miami is located" (p.
72). And, regarding Cuban Americans' respect for author-
ity, he states: "... the immigrant community impressed
Miami's law enforcers as singularly law-abiding. During
the early 1970s, the city's chief of police observed that
Cubans committed only 10 to 12 percent of all crimes although they accounted for a third of the population" (p.
83). Numerous clear black-and-white and a few color
photographs add interest and immediacy to the narrative.

Gillies, John. Señor Alcade: A Biography of Henry Cisneros.
Minneapolis: Dillon Press, Inc., 1988. 127 p. ISBN:
0-87518-374-3. $11.95. Gr. 5-7.

Admirers of the Mexican-American mayor of San Antonio,
Texas, will be pleased with this readable biography of
Henry Cisneros. In a simple style, the author describes
the Cisneros house, his growing up years, his work in
Washington, D.C., and his life as mayor. Numerous black-
and-white family photographs add interest to the mayor's
life. At the beginning, readers may be overwhelmed by
all the goodness in Cisneros life: "Henry was proud of
his family; his relatives were hard-working people who believed in freedom and democracy, as well as in education
and self-discipline. Over the years, Henry would learn to
apply these values to his own life" (p. 22). And, even
though the style is always highly complimentary, at least
towards the end the author does mention a few criticisms
regarding Cisneros' work. Some readers may be inspired

by Henry Cisneros' personal road map which, he feels, will help young people "who want to make the most of their educations and their future careers" (p. 99).

Gleiter, Jan, and Kathleen Thompson. David Farragut. Illustrated by Francis Balistreri. ISBN: 0-8172-2904-3.
_____. Diego Rivera. Illustrated by Yoshi Miyake. ISBN: 0-8172-2908-6.
_____. Junipero Serra. Illustrated by Charles Shaw. ISBN: 0-8172-2909-4.
Ea. vol.: 32 p. Milwaukee: Raintree Publishers, 1989. $15.99. Gr. 3-5.

The lives of three notable Hispanics from Mexico, the United States and Spain are briefly narrated in these bilingual (Spanish/English) books. Even though there is nothing particularly exciting about these titles, they do provide basic facts about the lives and accomplishments of these three Hispanic men who excelled in the U.S. Civil War, in the arts and in the development of missions in California. Unfortunately, these social study books will remind many readers of their textbooks, especially the bland watercolor illustrations and the lackluster Spanish and English texts. The context, however, is inspiring and true.

Gómez-Quiñones, Juan. Chicano Politics: Reality and Promise, 1940-1990. Albuquerque: University of New Mexico Press, 1990. 265 p. ISBN: 0-8263-1213-6 pap. $15.95. Gr. 10-adult.

Juan Gómez-Quiñones, a professor of history and a self-declared political activist, expresses his views regarding the political experience of Mexican Americans in the last fifty years. He explains that the basis for this study is "inquiry into the social relations of production" (p. 2) and blames prejudice for the "continued maintenance of the dominant Anglo American attitude of superiority toward Mexicans, a combination of ethnocentrism and supremacism" (p. 98). He believes that Mexican workers have confronted a whole series of injustices on the job market which have undermined their ability to secure meaningful well-being and concludes that "Mexicans must come to terms with the political process and social reality, and then deal with them as they are" (p. 214). Serious students of the political history of Mexican Americans will find this book interesting as well as challenging.

Gutman, Roy. Banana Diplomacy: The Making of American Policy in Nicaragua, 1981-1987. New York: Simon and Schuster, 1988. 404 p. ISBN: 0-671-60626-3. $19.95. Gr. 9-adult.

Based largely on personal interviews, Gutman provides a detailed report on the making of U.S. policy in Nicaragua during the Reagan administration. From the outset, he is critical of Reagan's foreign policy. He states: "A new team would be assembled to manage policy which had one thing in common: all its members lacked Latin American experience" (p. 27). And, from then on, the reader is exposed to what the author believes are all the mistakes, blunders, and misconceptions of the Reagan administration's policies and decisions regarding Nicaragua. Critics of Reagan's policies will certainly concur.

Hall, Douglas Kent. The Border: Life on the Line. New York: Abbeville Press Publishers, 1988. 251 p. ISBN: 0-89659-685-0. $35.00. Gr. 9-adult.

(See review under MEXICO.)

*Hall, Linda B., and Don M. Coerver. Revolution on the Border: the United States and Mexico, 1910-1920. Albuquerque: The University of New Mexico Press, 1988. 205 p. ISBN: 0-8263-1234-9. pap. $14.95. Gr. 9-adult.

The political, military, social and economic changes that took place on the border between Mexico and the United States between 1910 and 1920 are examined in this readable, well-organized narrative. In addition, it discusses the effects that these changes had on the Mexican Revolution and on the relations between the two countries. Twenty-four black-and-white photographs of the period add to readers' understanding of this difficult era in U.S.-

Mexico relations. This is indeed an excellent analysis of the many problems that have existed since 1910 and that persist to the present between the two countries.

Harlan, Judith. Hispanic Voters: A Voice in American Politics. New York: Franklin Watts, 1988. 112 p. ISBN: 0-531-10586-5. $12.90. Gr. 7-12.

Basic issues and concerns regarding Hispanic people in the U.S. are examined in this easy-to-read narrative. It discusses the backgrounds and politics of Mexican Americans, Puerto Ricans and Cubans especially as these affect such issues as bilingual education, English-only laws, immigration reform and national politics. This is a well-done introduction to Hispanics in the U.S. political scene.

*Hauser, Pierre N. Illegal Aliens. (The Peoples of North America) New York: Chelsea House Publishers, 1990. 127 p. ISBN: 0-87754-889-7. $17.95. Gr. 7-12.

With great insight and understanding, the author examines the history of undocumented immigration to the United States, the hardships endured by illegal aliens, their motives in immigrating, and current efforts to control illegal migration into the U.S. This is indeed a most realistic assessment of this difficult issue. The author's conclusion is, unfortunately, correct: "For now all that is certain about the problem of illegal aliens is that there is no easy solution" (p. 123). Even though some critics may disapprove, most of the book deals with illegal migrants from Mexico, who up to the 1970s represented 90 percent of all illegal aliens living in the U.S. And, even today, approximately 60 percent of the undocumented population is made up of Mexicans. Numerous photographs and wide margins add to the readability of this book.

Hernández, Irene Beltrán. Across the Great River. Houston: Arte Publico Press, 1989. 136 p. ISBN: 0-934770-96-4. $8.50. Gr. 7-10.

The hardships of a poor Mexican family, which crosses the border illegally into the United States, are narrated

through the eyes of Katarina, a young girl and the oldest
child. The story provides an intimate view of life by the
Rio Grande, including cruel labor smugglers, a kind folk
healer, and other "good" and "bad" characters. Some
readers will object to the story's much too simple ending,
but the constant action and true Mexican spirit will appeal
to other readers interested in a simple story about a
courageous little girl.

*Hewett, Joan. Getting Elected: The Diary of a Campaign.
Photos by Richard Hewett. New York: E. P. Dutton,
1989. 48 p. ISBN: 0-525-67259-1. $13.95. Gr. 4-8.

In a matter-of-fact and easy-to-understand manner, the
author describes the political campaign of Gloria Molina, a
Mexican American, who seeks election to the Los Angeles
City Council. Black-and-white photographs on every page
as well as a direct narrative convey the excitement, hard-
work and serious organization that surround the election
process in a political campaign. This book is especially
informative to new Hispanic immigrants, who, for the most
part, are not familiar with the inner workings of a democracy

Hewett, Joan. Hector Lives in the United States Now: The
Story of a Mexican-American Child. Photos by Richard
Hewett. New York: J. B. Lippincott, 1990. 42 p.
ISBN: 0-397-32295-X. $13.95. Gr. 3-6.

Through Hector, a Mexican-American boy who lives in Los
Angeles, readers are exposed to the daily life of a Mexican-
American family as well as to two important events in their
lives: first communion and legal residency in the United
States through the Immigration Reform and Control Act.
Black-and-white photos of Hector and his family provide
a close look at their numerous activities.

*Hulbert, Jay, and Sid Kantor. Armando Asked, "Why?"
(Ready, Set, Read) Illustrated by Pat Hogan. Milwaukee:
Raintree Publishers, 1990. 24 p. ISBN: 0-8172-35676-0.
$12.33. Gr. K-2.

Armando, a Hispanic boy, is always asking "Why?" and his

family is always too busy to answer his questions. One
day they take him to the library, introduce him to the librarian, and find many books to answer his questions.
The conclusion of this story may not be very satisfying
and a bit contrived, but the Hispanic family, including a
kindly grandmother, are appealing and could definitely serve
as role models. (Because grandmother is addressed as
"Nana," many would call this a Puerto Rican family. But
grandmothers are also called "nanas" in other Hispanic
families.)

James, Betsy. The Dream Stair. Illustrated by Richard
Jesse Watson. New York: Harper & Row, Publishers, 1990.
[30 p.] ISBN: 0-06-022788-5. $13.95. Gr. 1-3.

A young girl poetically relates her thoughts and dreams
about going to bed at night and having a granny to kiss
her good night and to hug her in the morning. Beautiful
full-color illustrations of a Hispanic girl, her grandmother
and numerous Hispanic motifs make this a special story
about traveling up and down a dream staircase.

Langley, Lester D. MexAmerica: Two Countries, One Future.
New York: Crown Publishers, Inc., 1988. 312 p. ISBN:
0-517-56732-6. $19.95. Gr. 10-adult.

The author describes this as an "impressionistic and personal account" which explores the impact of Mexican culture on American society. He offers interesting perspec-
tives on various issues surrounding Mexican Americans in
the U.S., such as the debate about making English the
official language, the problem of Mexican immigrants and
bilingualism. The first part of the book concentrates on
U.S. cities with a large Mexican-American population:
Chicago, Houston, San Antonio, Denver, Kansas City,
San Diego and Los Angeles. The second part describes
his travels and experiences in three Mexican cities: Monterrey, Guadalajara and Mexico City. The author's insights
on the life of Mexican Americans in the U.S. are amusing
and, at times, enlightening. On the other hand, his observations about life in Mexico are much more limited and
constricted. For example, about Mexico City he states:
"In five visits to Mexico City I have never met anyone,

from street-sweeper and beggar to small businessman or
petty government official ... who liked anything about
Mexico City" (p. 236). Millions of people in Mexico City
will certainly disagree.

*Larsen, Ronald J. The Puerto Ricans in America. Min-
neapolis: Lerner Publications Company, 1989. 76 p.
ISBN: 0-8225-0238-0. $8.95; ISBN: 0-8225-1036-7. pap.
$3.95. Gr. 6-9.

The history and life of Puerto Ricans in the United States
are narrated through a most readable text with black-and-
white photographs on almost every page. This is an outstanding overview of the land and people of Puerto Rico
with additional chapters on migration to and life on U.S.
mainland, political and community organizations, and Puerto
Ricans on the mainland who have made important contributions to American life and culture.

*Long, Jeff. Duel of Eagles: The Mexican and U.S. Fight
for the Alamo. New York: William Morrow and Company,
1990. 431 p. ISBN: 0-688-07252-6. $22.95. Gr. 9-
adult.

All the negative sides of both the American and Mexican
"heroes" and leaders of the incidents that led to the fight
for the Alamo as well as the events that followed it are
related in a passionate and most entertaining manner in
this well-documented historical narrative. The following
is an example of how Long describes William Barret Travis,
one of Texas' well-known leaders: "Texas was spinning
with men like Travis.... He became his own creation: a
womanizer, a gambler, a gallant gentleman, and a martyr-
rebel. There were ten or more men for every woman in
Texas. Yet somehow, by the age of twenty-four, Travis
had slept with over fifty frontier belles, slave girls, and
prostitutes" (p. 34). Of course, Mexico's military ruler
and chief executive, Antonio López de Santa Anna, "was
a coward who more than once abandoned his army and ran
from the enemy" (p. 85). And, "Santa Anna was an opium
addict.... In certain respects, both of these substance
abusers manifested remarkably similar behavior during their
war with each other" (p. 146). Some readers may disagree

with the author's candid description of people and events during the battle for Texas. Nevertheless, this is indeed fascinating reading that will bore no one.

Martínez, Max. <u>Schoolland</u>. Houston, TX: Arte Publico Press, University of Houston, 1988. 250 p. ISBN: 0-934770-87-5. $8.50. Gr. 9-adult.

The daily life of a Mexican-American family in rural Texas during the 1950s is described through the eyes of an adolescent boy. In a frank manner and with strong language, a teenager tells about his family's drinking habits, attitudes toward "whites" and wetbacks as well as his feelings about girls and other problems of growing up. This is not a simple novel for adolescents, but rather a deeply felt novel about life in small towns and farms in Texas.

Martínez, Oscar J. <u>Troublesome Border</u>. Tucson: University of Arizona Press, 1988. 177 p. ISBN: 0-8165-1033-4. $22.95. Gr. 9-adult.

Martínez, professor of history at the University of Texas, El Paso, states that this book is about conflict in the U.S.-Mexico border and that his intent "is not to present a comprehensive history of that subject but rather to examine selected topics that illuminate ... relationships in the borderlands" (p. xi). Thus, after reviewing the history of the border region, he discusses the social, economic and cultural predicaments of the people in the area. In a forceful manner, Martínez blames "distasteful U.S. policy decisions" (p. 26) and U.S. expansionist aggressions for taking advantage of its weaker neighbor and condemning Mexico "to diminished wealth, a scarcity of agricultural land, and limited economic growth" (p. 30). In the chapter, "Border Indians," Martínez argues that as a "result of a war of conquest, Indians and Chicanos were involuntarily incorporated into the United States ... both groups became second-class citizens in American society" (p. 79). This is a vigorous indictment against high-level U.S. policy makers. Some will undoubtedly concur; others will certainly disagree.

Mayberry, Jodine. Mexicans. (Recent American Immigrants)
New York: Franklin Watts, 1990. 64 p. ISBN: 0-531-
10979-8. $12.40. Gr. 5-8.

Briefly and succinctly, the author discusses the history
of Mexicans and Mexican Americans, their reasons for immigrating to the U.S., their lifestyles and contributions
to their new country. Numerous black-and-white and
color photographs as well as the narrative emphasize the
discrimination, poverty and abuse that many Mexicans have
endured in the U.S. In addition, it discusses other serious problems of Mexicans in the U.S., such as the high
educational dropout rate and Chicano youth gangs.

Meier, Matt S. Mexican American Biographies: A Historical
Dictionary, 1836-1987. New York: Greenwood Press,
1988. 270 p. ISBN: 0-313-24521-5. $45.00. Gr. 9-
adult.

The author attempted to identify and provide basic information on prominent Mexican-American figures from the
period of the Texas revolution in the mid-1830s to the
present time. Even though 200 of the 270 entries are of
contemporary Mexican Americans, there are innumerable
omissions which seriously detract from the value of this
expensive biographical dictionary. The author explains
that in the area "of contemporary Chicano 'prominentes' a
special problem arose in some cases. Letters sent to many
of them requesting biographical information went unanswered" (p. viii). This is indeed regrettable, but it
does limit the usefulness of this dictionary as a reference
tool about contemporary prominent Mexican Americans.

Mendheim, Beverly. Ritchie Valens, the First Latino Rocker.
Tempe, AZ: Bilingual Press, 1987. 160 p. ISBN: 0-
916950-79-4. $10.00. Gr. 9-adult.

The author states that the purpose of this book is "to
tell the story of a very unique individual, who rose from
the poverty of a Los Angeles barrio to become a musical
phenomenon" (p. 13). In a plain style, she relates the
musical experiences in the life of Ritchie Valens as well as
the factors that shaped those experiences. Music lovers

will not be disappointed in this readable yet serious report of the "first successful Chicano rock and roller"
also known as the "father" of Latin/Chicano rock.

*Neugeboren, Jay. Poli, a Mexican Boy in Early Texas. Il-
lustrated by Tom Leamon. San Antonio, TX: Corona
Publishing Company, 1989. 123 p. ISBN: 0-931722-72-1.
$13.95. Gr. 6-8.

José Policarpo Rodriguez, later known as "Poli," came with
his father from Mexico to the Republic of Texas in 1839.
Through his father, Poli became friendly with the
Comanches and learned about life in Texas from the Mexicans, Indians and Anglos. In a fast-moving fictionalized
account, the author describes what "life was like for
Mexicans and Texans, and especially for Mexican-Texans
who grew up and came of age with the State of Texas
during its formative years, from 1839 to 1846" (p. xi).
Young readers will definitely enjoy the excitement and adventure in Poli's life. At the same time, they will learn
that Poli was the best scout Texas Ranger Capt. Jack
Hayes ever had, the first Mexican American commissioned
in the Rangers and other notable achievements. The author
takes several artistic liberties in describing life in Mexico
in the nineteenth century. Nonetheless, this is a compelling story about an honest, courageous and sensitive
Mexican boy in early Texas.

Ochoa, George. The Fall of Mexico City

(See review under MEXICO.)

Parsons, Jack. Straight from the Heart: Portraits of Traditional Hispanic Musicians. Photographs by the author.
Albuquerque: University of New Mexico Press, 1990.
93 p. ISBN: 0-8263-1217-9. pap. $17.50. Gr. 9-
adult.

Fifty-two black-and-white photographs of Hispanic musicians from New Mexico and Colorado and a thirty-three-
page essay that describes the evolution of Hispanic folk
music in this area are included in this publication. Serious

students of folk music will be interested in the passion, tradition and natural environment of Hispanic musicians so movingly depicted by this author/photographer.

*Pinchot, Jane. The Mexicans in America. Minneapolis: Lerner Publications Company, 1989. 94 p. ISBN: 0-8225-1016-2. pap. $3.95. ISBN: 0-8225-0222-4. $8.95. Gr. 6-9.

The history and life of Mexicans in the United States are narrated through a straightforward text and black-and-white photographs on every page. This is indeed an excellent overview of the origins of the American Southwest and the difficulties that Mexican Americans have experienced in education, employment, property rights and politics. It also includes a chapter on the contributions of Mexican Americans to the life and culture in the United States.

*Portes, Alejandro, and Rubén G. Rumbaut. Immigrant America: A Portrait. Berkeley: University of California Press, 1990. 300 p. ISBN: 0-520-06894-7. $39.95. ISBN: 0-520-07038-0. pap. $10.95. Gr. 10-adult.

This is an excellent portrait of recent immigration to the United States that is both comprehensive and comprehensible. The focus is on the diversity of the origins, adaptation and experiences of today's immigrants. The authors must be commended for discussing controversial issues regarding immigration into the U.S. with much objectivity and a high degree of scholarship without the political rhetoric that usually accompanies this topic. Educators will find a most valuable discussion on the current evidence regarding bilingual education on chapter 6, "Learning the Ropes: Language and the Second Generation." The following statement may serve as a summary of the authors' positive conclusions: "Overall, immigration has been and will continue to be positive for the country both in terms of filling labor needs at different levels of the economy and, more important, injecting into society the energies, ambitions and skills of positively selected groups" (p. 26).

Prieto, Jorge. Harvest of Hope: The Pilgrimage of a Mexican-
American Physician. Notre Dame, IN: University of
Notre Dame Press, 1989. 157 p. ISBN: 0-268-01087-0.
$20.95. Gr. 9-adult.

Jorge Prieto, a physician and past president of the Chicago Board of Health, relates his life in Mexico and the
United States in this moving autobiography. Readers will
be especially touched by Dr. Prieto's early experiences as
a young doctor in a poor village in central Mexico. Later
he describes his life as a doctor in Cook County Hospital
in Chicago where, he states: "This was my first exposure
to institutionalized racism" (p. 64). The most interesting
parts of this book are the ones that deal with various aspects of the medical profession--the education, residency
and practice of medicine. Some readers might share the
author's religious beliefs and hence be moved by his devotion to his religion. Others might be interested in reading about the successes of a dedicated Mexican-American
doctor. Overall, this is an inspiring autobiography with
activist messages.

Recuerdos de los viejitos/Tales of the Rio Puerco. Collected
and edited by Nasario García. Albuquerque: University
of New Mexico Press, 1987. 266 p. ISBN: 0-8263-1021-4.
$9.95. Gr. 9-adult.

Sixty-four tales related in the Spanish vernacular by the
Hispanics of the Rio Puerco Valley in west-central New
Mexico and their English translations are included in this
publication. It includes tales about the supernatural as
well as the people and their tragedies, religion, misfor-
tunes. The brevity and simplicity of these tales may
appeal to readers interested in the folklore of New Mexico;
however, the extensive use of Spanish archaisms, regional-
isms, Anglicisms and idiomatic expressions limit the appeal
of these tales.

Rice, James. Texas Jack at the Alamo. Illustrated by the
author. Gretna, LA: Pelican Publishing Company, 1989.
[30 p.] ISBN: 0-88289-725-X. $11.95. Gr. 3-5.

Texas Jack, a long-eared jackrabbit, simply re-

counts the battle of the Alamo in 1836 emphasizing the
bravery of Davy Crockett, Jim Bowie and Colonel William
Travis. Of special interest are the color and black-and-
white illustrations which vividly recreate the battle and
life inside the fort as it was in 1836. The jackrabbit's
witty comments add a light touch to this tragic event in
Texas history, which may be missed by young readers.

*Schoberle, Cecile. Esmeralda and the Pet Parade. New
York: Simon and Schuster, Inc., 1990. [32 p.] ISBN:
0-671-67958-9. $14.95. Gr. 2-4.

Esmeralda, Juan's boisterous pet goat, is always getting
in trouble. She eats the flowers, pulls down Mama's clean
laundry, and knocks over the trash can. So, when Juan
decides to dress up Esmeralda for the pet parade, all the
family warns him not to let her spoil their chances of
winning. Lively linoleum block prints with appropriate
Southwestern illustrations beautifully complement this warm
story about a Hispanic boy, his adorable goat and his
understanding grandfather.

Soto, Gary. Who Will Know Us? San Francisco: Chronicle
Books, 1990. 69 p. ISBN: 0-87701-673-9. pap. $8.95.
Gr. 9-adult.

In a quiet, poetic, yet conversational manner, Soto describes his childhood, travels, family, everyday life and
memories in this collection of forty-one poems. Poetry
lovers, especially Mexican-American readers, will empathize
with these poetic vignettes about "Fat Man and a Pool-
side Weekend," "Looking for a Cemetery," "Good Morning,
Fresno" and others.

Stanek, Muriel. I Speak English for My Mom. Illustrated by
Judith Friedman. Niles, IL: Albert Whitman & Company,
1989. [32 p.] ISBN: 0-8075-3659-8. $10.50. Gr. 3-5.

Lupe, a Mexican-American girl, must translate for her mother who speaks only Spanish. They are shown going to the
doctor, talking to Lupe's teacher, using the telephone,
going to the store and other necessary activities where Lupe

must help her mother. Finally, Lupe's mom decides to
learn English so that she can get a better job. Somewhat
stilted black-and-white pencil illustrations complement the
easy-to-read text. This is a realistic story about a
Mexican-American girl and her mother who work and study
hard in their new country. It must be noted that this
story emphasizes what many Anglos believe Hispanics must
do in their new country, thus detracting from the true
values and beliefs of most Mexican-American families. Of
course, most Hispanics in the U.S. want to learn English,
but this is not the key to their existence, as this story
implies.

*Warren, Nancy Hunter. <u>Villages of Hispanic New Mexico</u>.
Santa Fe, NM: School of American Research Press, 1987.
111 p. ISBN: 0-933452-20-9. $14.95. Gr. 8-adult.

In a sensitive and lucid manner, the author/photographer
offers a glimpse into the life and people of Hispanic villages
in northern and central New Mexico. Readers interested
in the history, religion, villages, landscapes, feast days
and other aspects of life in this area of New Mexico will
not be disappointed. Numerous excellent black-and-white
photographs, taken in the 1970s, are informative as well
as aesthetically pleasing.

West, John O. <u>Mexican-American Folklore</u>. Little Rock, AR:
August House, Inc., 1988. 314 p. ISBN: 0-87483-059-1.
$9.95. Gr. 9-adult.

The editor/compiler has put together a wide representation
of Mexican-American folklore from the American Southwest.
It includes chapters on folk speech, proverbs, riddles,
rhymes, prose narrative, ballads and folksongs, beliefs
and superstitions, customs, folk drama, folk games, folk
architecture, foods and crafts. There are two things that
make this book less than desirable: 1) Too many of the
words in Spanish are misspelled, e.g., "nácio" and "nacío"
[sic] (p. 37), "refránes" [sic] (p. 39), "alacránes" [sic]
(p. 40), "platano" [sic] (p. 50); 2) Most of the black-and-
white photographs are unclear or poor quality.

*Woods, Geraldine. <u>Affirmative Action</u>. New York: Franklin Watts, 1989. 128 p. ISBN: 0-531-10657-8. $12.90. Gr. 9-12.

In a clear and readable manner, the author describes the history, pros, cons and future of affirmative action in the United States. It discusses such difficult questions as, Why have the courts ruled both in favor and against affirmative action in different cases? Who benefits from affirmative action? This is a balanced discussion of many of the complex issues regarding affirmative action today.

URUGUAY

Uruguay in Pictures. Text by Nathan A. Haverstock. (Visual Geography Series) Minneapolis: Lerner Publications Company, 1987. 64 p. ISBN: 0-8225-1823-6. $9.95. Gr. 6-10.

The geography, history, government, people and economy of this small South American country are presented in this basic guide. Numerous black-and-white and color photographs add much interest to the informative text. The following paragraph illustrates the objective tone of this publication: "The absence of extremes of wealth or poverty in Uruguay gives the nation's three million people a basically middle-class outlook. Despite some economic hardships since the mid-twentieth century, most Uruguayans enjoy adequate food, housing, and medical care. The nation's cities have fewer slums than most Latin American countries, and only the poorest city dwellers lack electricity, running water, and sewers" (p. 42).

VENEZUELA

*Gutiérrez, Douglas. The Night of the Stars. Illustrated by
María Fernandez Oliver. Translated from the Spanish by
Carmen Diana Dearden. New York: Kane/Miller Book
Publishers, 1988. [24 p.] ISBN: 0-916291-170. $9.95.
Gr. 2-4.

This story, originally published in Venezuela in 1987, tells
about a man who does not like the darkness of night and
finds a way to bring some light to nighttime. The charming watercolor illustrations subtly portray life in a small
village in Venezuela.

Lye, Keith. Take a Trip to Venezuela. New York: Franklin
Watts, Inc., 1988. 32 p. ISBN: 0-531-10469-9. $9.90.
Gr. 2-4.

Basic information about the geography, people, history,
cities and industries of Venezuela is provided through an
easy-to-read text and color photographs on every page,
This is, unfortunately, an unexciting yet basic introduction to this South American country with such trite statements as "... new wealth can be created by hard work
and the founding of new industries" (p. 30).

*Morrison, Marion. Venezuela. (Enchantment of the World)
Chicago: Childrens Press, 1989. 128 p. ISBN: 0-516-
02711-5. $16.95. Gr. 5-8.

Outstanding photographs in color and a readable text introduce readers to the history, geography, people, culture

and economy of Venezuela. As opposed to many books that discuss life in Latin America, this one does an excellent job in reporting the marked contrasts prevalent in many areas of living, learning and working in Venezuela. The mini-facts section provides additional information in a well-organized manner.

Venezuela in Pictures. (Visual Geography Series) Minneapolis: Lerner Publications Company, 1987. 64 p. ISBN: 0-8225-1824-4. $9.95. Gr. 5-10.

Like other titles in this series, this one introduces the reader to the land, history, government, people and economy of Venezuela in a direct and straightforward manner. Numerous black-and-white and color photographs add to the reader's understanding of various aspects of this South American country. The editors must be commended for describing with much objectivity such difficult issues as governmental corruption and the contrasts between rich and poor.

AUTHOR INDEX

(Including co-authors and editors)

TITLE INDEX

SUBJECT INDEX

Venezia, Picasso 97

Walker, Pride of Puerto Rico: The Life of Roberto
Clemente 86

White, The Story of Junípero Serra, Brave Adventurer
98

Zamora, Frida Kahlo: The Brush of Anguish 66

BOLIVIA
Blair, The Land and People of Bolivia 4
Martin, Bolivia 7
Morrison, Bolivia 8

BOLIVIA--Children
Martin, Bolivia 7

CANSECO, JOSE
Aaseng, Jose Canseco: Baseball's 40-40 Man 99

CARIBBEAN--Fiction
Michener, Caribbean 43

CARIBBEAN--History
Black, The Good Neighbor: How the United States Wrote
the History of Central America and the Caribbean 10

CASTRO, FIDEL
Vail, Fidel Castro 23

CENTRAL AMERICA
(See also Latin America, Costa Rica, El Salvador, Guatemala, Honduras, Nicaragua, and Panama)

CENTRAL AMERICA--Fiction
Czernecki, The Time Before Dreams 10

CENTRAL AMERICA--Folklore
Czernecki, The Time Before Dreams 10

CENTRAL AMERICA--History
Black, The Good Neighbor: How the United States Wrote
the History of Central America and the Caribbean 10

CENTRAL AMERICA--Mythology
Bierhorst, The Mythology of Mexico and Central America
49

Pinchot, The Mexicans in America 118
Staneck, I Speak English for My Mom 120

MEXICAN AMERICANS--Women
Hewett, Getting Elected: The Diary of a Campaign 112

MEXICO
Calderwood and Baeña, Mexico, a Higher Vision: An
Aerial Journey from Past to Present 49
Clarke, Travels in Mexico and California: Comprising a
Journal of a Tour from Brazos Santiago. Through
Central Mexico, by Way of Monterrey, Chihuahua, the
Country of the Apaches, and the River Gila to the
Mining Districts of California 51
Davis, Mexico City 52
Desmond and Messenger, A Dream of Maya: Augustus
and Alice Le Plongeon in Nineteenth-Century Yucatan
52
Haskins, Count Your Way Through Mexico 57
James, Inside Mexico 57

MEXICO--Architecture and Interior Design
Street-Porter, Casa Mexicana 65

MEXICO--Art
Berdan, The Aztecs 48
Zamora, Frida Kahlo: The Brush of Anguish 66

MEXICO--Aztecs
Bateman, Aztecs and Incas: AD 1300-1532 47
Berdan, The Aztecs 48
Berler, The Conquest of Mexico: A Modern Rendering
of William H. Prescott's History 48
Fisher, Pyramid of the Sun, Pyramid of the Moon 53
Gleiter and Thompson, Diego Rivera 55
Lattimore, The Flame of Peace: A Tale of the Aztecs 58
Odijk, The Aztecs 60
Rohmer and Anchondo, How We Came to the Fifth World/
Cómo vinimos al quinto mundo: A Creation Story from
Ancient Mexico 85
Steel, An Aztec Warrior 65

MEXICO--Biography
Desmond, A Dream of Maya: Augustus and Alice Le Plongeon in Nineteenth-Century Yucatan 52

Bierhorst, The Mythology of South America   39

Lattimore, The Flame of Peace: A Tale of the Aztecs
   58

Lattimore, Why There Is No Arguing in Heaven: A Mayan
   Myth   58

Rohmer and Anchondo, How We Came to the Fifth World/
   Cómo vinimos al quinto mundo: A Creation Story from
   Ancient Mexico   85

Schele and Freidel, A Forest of Kings: The Untold Story
   of the Ancient Maya   64

Shetterly, The Dwarf-Wizard of Uxmal   64

NICARAGUA
   Lye, Take a Trip to Nicaragua   70

NICARAGUA--Children
   Cummins, Nicaragua   67
   DeSauza, Brother Anansi and the Cattle Ranch/El hermano
      Anansi y el rancho de ganado   68

NICARAGUA--Family Life
   Cummins, Nicaragua   67

NICARAGUA--Fiction
   DeSauza, Brother Anansi and the Cattle Ranch/El hermano
      Anansi y el rancho de ganado   68
   Rohmer and Wilson, Mother scorpion Country/La tierra de
      la Madre Escorpión   70

NICARAGUA--Folklore
   Rohmer, Chow, and Vidaure, The Invisible Hunters/Los
      cazadores invisibles   71
   Rohmer, Uncle Nacho's Hat/El sombreto de tío Nacho   70

NICARAGUA--History
   Jenkins, Nicaragua and the United States   69

NICARAGUA--Miskito Indians
   Rohmer, Chow, and Vidaure, The Invisible Hunters/Los
      cazadores invisibles   71
   Rohmer and Wilson, Mother Scorpion Country/La tierra de
      la Madre Escorpión   70

NICARAGUA--People
   Lye, Take a Trip to Nicaragua   70